Johnny Appleseed

A VOICE IN THE WILDERNESS

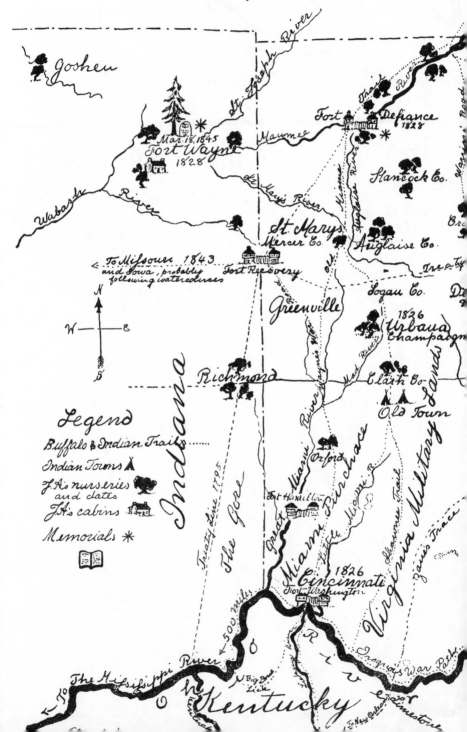

Lake Erie

great Iroquois Trail

Cleveland

Western Reserve
(to Connecticut)

Sandusky

FIRE LANDS
Huron Co.
1811

Pennsylvania

Fort Duquesne Pittsburgh

Ashland
Ashland Co.

Fort Laurens

Mansfield
Richland Co.
1814

Mt Vernon
Knox Co.

Cos-hoc-ton

Tuscarawas

Steubenville
Jefferson Co.
1806

Seven Ranges

Reserve R.

Newark

Licking

Road

Zanesville
1800

Zane's Trace
old buffalo trail
Dexter City

Wheeling

To Potomac R.

Owl Creek

Owl Creek 1800

Tuscarawas River

Muskingum River

Ohio Company

Marietta

Chapman home 1805

Blennerhasset Island

Chillicothe

Scioto River

icothe

Virginia

Ohio

Kanawha River

La Salle 1670

"Johnny Appleseed"
his Map
of the Ohio Country
Compiled & sketched
by friends
1945

Johnny Appleseed

A VOICE IN THE WILDERNESS

The Story of the Pioneer
John Chapman

A TRIBUTE

Editor
William Ellery Jones

Chrysalis Books
West Chester, Pennsylvania

First edition, 1945, "Centennial Tribute," The Swedenborg Press, Patterson, N.J.; second edition, 1946; third edition, 1947; fourth edition, "Memorial Highway Edition," 1953; fifth edition, 1957; sixth edition, 1966, Johnny Appleseed Memorial Library, Cincinnati, Ohio
Seventh edition, 2000, Swedenborg Foundation, West Chester, Pennsylvania

Library of Congress Cataloging-in-Publication Data

Johnny Appleseed : a voice in the wilderness : the story of the pioneer John Chapman : a tribute / editor, William Ellery Jones.—7th ed.
    p. cm.
  Includes bibliographical references.
  ISBN 0-87785-304-5
  1. Appleseed, Johnny, 1774–1845. 2. Apple growers—United States—Biography. 3. Frontier and pioneer life—Middle West. I. Jones, William Ellery.

SB63.C46 J59 2000
634′.11′092—dc21
[B]   00-056950

Designed by Sans Serif, Inc.
Typeset in Galliard by Sans Serif, Inc., Saline, Michigan
Printed in the United States of America

Chrysalis Books is an imprint of the Swedenborg Foundation, Inc. For more information, contact:
    Chrysalis Books
    Swedenborg Foundation
    320 North Church Street
    West Chester, PA 19380
            or
    http://www.swedenborg.com

CONTENTS

CONTENTS

—— 🌳 ——

FOREWORD TO FIRST EDITION

The most gracious and heart-warming legend to grow up in America is that of Johnny Appleseed. In general, legend-making in America has turned to the wild exaggeration and raucous humor of the Paul Bunyan type. The magnitude and frontier crudeness of life in this rapidly expanding nation has seemed to direct the imagination of the people toward the gigantesque rather than toward the quiet and the gentle. It is significant, however, that Paul Bunyan is not honored by monuments or by spontaneous celebrations and pageants of school children. That is a distinction reserved for the beloved memory of humble, kindly Johnny Appleseed.

His is a beautiful legend, and it is still taking shape before our modern eyes. Its essential characteristics are now thoroughly familiar to all of us. They were dramatically set forth in the folklore exhibit at the New York World's Fair in 1939. The gentle saint of the Ohio–Indiana frontier was represented in bas-relief as a bearded prophet whose eyes are fixed on supernal things. With his mush pan on his head, with one hand scattering apple seeds upon the good earth and the other holding a Swedenborgian book of prophecy, the barefooted Johnny Appleseed strides effortlessly across the country doing good to the souls and the bodies of his fellow humans and to all God's creatures.

We turn our minds back to the frontier out of which this legend emerged. We think of the sickening barbarism of the Indian wars: of the torture of Colonel William

Crawford, of the horrible massacre of the Moravian Indians, of the murder of Old Briton and the Indian feast on his boiled flesh, of the terrorism of the Girty Brothers. . . . We remember the grim and solitary lives of men and women on lonely farms in the wilderness. And we reflect upon the elemental need deep in the hearts of men which, in such surroundings, erects out of its own longing the figure of Johnny Appleseed to keep alive the precious qualities of gentleness, kindliness, peace, and good will upon the earth.

Thanks to scholars like Dr. Robert Price, the facts about John Chapman have been brought to light. It is now possible, momentarily at least, to divest him of his legend and see him as a man born as other men, moving west to do business as a nurseryman and a recognized missionary, and making a modest success in his venture. I have met many people, and have had correspondence with more, who object to, even resist, this activity of the scholars. They say it is wrong to damage or undermine the legend with these prosaic researches. But they are wrong. Gathering the facts about John Chapman does not detract from Johnny Appleseed—far from it. His legend is enhanced thereby. There is magic in it. We are too far away from the flesh-and-blood Joseph ever to see him apart from his legend which submerges him in the great tribal mythos of his famine-stricken and exiled people and makes him so much greater than himself. And Saint Francis, too, has become completely absorbed in his inspiring legend. But the transformation of John Chapman into Johnny Appleseed is still visible, as the material in this volume so engagingly shows.

Our interest in John Chapman, the nurseryman and evangelist, and in Johnny Appleseed, the St. Francis of the frontier, has never been brighter than it is at present. The more we learn of John Chapman and his work, the firmer and larger grows the figure of Johnny Appleseed. New apple trees that he is said to have planted spring up in unexpected places, new stories of his tenderness, his benevolence, and his supernatural powers are born from the longing of the folk mind for these qualities in a strife-torn and warring world. He is a fertile subject for fable, poetry, fiction, and art. His legend is not yet fully fashioned, and his spirit strides over the Ohio and Indiana cornfields, over the orchards and farms, where John Chapman walked and labored in the wilderness a century ago. It is fitting that this modest tribute should be paid to his immortality on the centenary of his death.

HARLAN HATCHER
1945

PREFATORY NOTES

Preface 1

Excerpt from *Journal of the Proceedings of the Fifth General Convention of the Receivers of the Doctrines of the New Jerusalem,* held at the Temple, in the city of Philadelphia, on Monday, June 3, 1822, and continued until Wednesday, June 5.

Page 7 (quoting from a report by) The committee appointed to select from the communications on the subject of the church such parts as it may be useful to publish. . . . In the state of Ohio throughout, the great work is going on still more extensively. Besides the society established at Steubenville . . . and Lebanon and the very numerous church of Cincinnati . . . one very extraordinary missionary continues to exert, for the spread of divine truth his modest and humble efforts, which would put the most zealous members to the blush. We now allude to Mr. John Chapman, from whom we are in the habit of hearing frequently. His temporal employment consists in preceding the settlements, and sowing nurseries of fruit trees, which he avows to be pursued for the chief purpose of giving him an opportunity of spreading the doctrines throughout the western country. In his progress, which neither heat nor cold, swamps nor mountains, are permitted to arrest, he carries on his back all the New Church publications he can procure, and distributes them wherever opportunity is afforded. So great is his zeal, that he does not hesitate to divide his volumes into parts, and by repeated calls, enable the readers to peruse the whole in succession. Having no family, and inured to hardships of every kind, his operations are unceasing. He is now employed in traversing the district between Detroit and the closer settlements of Ohio. What shall be the reward of such an individual, where, as we are told in holy writ, *they that turn many to righteousness shall shine as the stars forever.—"*

Preface 2

From a report of the *Society for Printing, Publishing and Circulating the Writings of Emanuel Swedenborg,* Manchester, England, January 14, 1817.

There is in the western country a very extraordinary missionary of the New Jerusalem. A man has appeared who seems to be almost independent of corporeal wants and sufferings. He goes barefooted, can sleep anywhere, in house or out of house, and live upon the coarsest and most scanty fare. He has actually thawed the ice with his bare feet.

He procures what books he can of the New Church, travels into the remote settlements, and lends them wherever he can find readers, and sometimes divides a book into two or three parts for more extensive distribution and usefulness. This man for years past has been in the employment of bringing into cultivation, in numberless places in the wilderness, small patches (two or three acres) of ground, and then sowing apple seeds and rearing nurseries.

These become valuable as the settlements approximate, and the profits of the whole are intended for the purpose of enabling him to print all the writings of Emanuel

Swedenborg, and distribute them through the western settlements of the United States."

Preface 3

Honoring Johnny Appleseed, the United States Post Office announced it would issue a 5¢ postage stamp, September 24, 1966, commemorating his life and work as having a significant place in the lore of pioneer Americans in some national field of work.

For the first time, Johnny Appleseed, listed as John Chapman, of course, has been given a place in *Who Was Who* (New York: 1966). He is named as an American folk hero.

ACKNOWLEDGMENTS

Many people have aided me in my research, and some have brought certain information to my attention. For their contributions, I am especially grateful to the following:

> Mary Jane Henney; Maxine Kinton; Karen Furlong of the Mansfield-Richland County Public Library in Mansfield, Ohio; Robert Carter; Alan Wigton of the Little Journeys Bookshop in Mansfield; Mr. and Mrs. Robert Thornburg; Steven Fortriede of the Allen County Public Library in Fort Wayne, Indiana; Thomas Aquinas Burke of the Ohio Historical Society Library in Columbus, Ohio; George Blaine Huff; Hugh Durbin of the Urbana University Library in Urbana, Ohio; Reverend and Mrs. Norman Bestor; the Reverend Eric Allison; the staff of Cincinnati Historical Society Library; Tom Neel of the Ohio Genealogical Society in Mansfield; Sally Maier of the Shelby Museum of History; Dr. Elizabeth Reed; the staff of the Ashland Public Library; David Ferree and Diane Miller of the Ohio Agricultural Research & Development Center in Wooster, Ohio; and Richard DeLauder.

And special thanks go to Deborah Forman and Susan Flagg Poole of the Swedenborg Foundation in West Chester, Pennsylvania, for agreeing to reprint this book; and to Mary Lou Bertucci for her editorial assistance. But my deepest gratitude goes to my wife, Vickie Putney Jones, of WVXU Radio in Cincinnati, for her many years of patience and enthusiasm.

WILLIAM ELLERY JONES

INTRODUCTION

Why reprint a book about Johnny Appleseed that was first published in 1945? Because it is still historically significant. *Johnny Appleseed: A Voice in the Wilderness* was, at its initial printing, the first serious historical anthology of its kind ever compiled about the man John Chapman.

Previous accounts had been mostly fiction, or fiction mixed with fact, or county and state histories that repeated similar rhetoric. The present work, however, will always be a classic because it is a product of its time. Although previous editions were printed in 1945, 1946, 1947, 1953, 1957, and 1966, little new information about John Chapman has surfaced since the first edition. Much of what has been discovered is included in the "Editor's Update," which will be found at the end of each of the original essays. With an additional chapter and expanded resource list, this seventh edition is an even stronger and more reliable resource for educators, historians, the casual biography reader, and members of the Swedenborgian faith.

The heightened focus on Johnny "Appleseed" Chapman during development of the first edition evolved from several dynamic forces at work simultaneously. Robert Price, whose articles already were stimulating a renewed interest in Chapman nationally, had previously written *John Chapman: A Bibliography of Johnny Appleseed in History, Literature and Folklore* for the Swedenborg Press in 1944 and was known to be working on a much larger biography of Chapman. World War II heightened the country's need to reflect on its history's earlier heroes, who also dealt with what appeared to be insurmountable challenges. And the year 1945 represented the centennial commemoration of John Chapman's death.

Johnny Appleseed: A Voice in the Wilderness was written and compiled by authors who loved, admired, and respected their subject—and they commanded respect themselves.

Harlan Hatcher had previously included Johnny Appleseed in his work *The Buckeye Country* (New York: H. C. Kinsey & Co., 1940). His scholarly research focused on American literature and history, particularly of the Midwest. Hatcher's career in education included his serving as vice-president of Ohio State University and as president of the University of Michigan.

Robert Price was a rural school teacher and country newspaper reporter in the Midwest before being graduated from Denison University. After receiving M.A. and PH.D. degrees from Ohio State University, he served as professor of English at Otterbein College in Westerville, Ohio. By the time *A Voice in the Wilderness* appeared, Price had already secured a grant in aid to complete his larger study of John Chapman, which he finished in 1947. He published his definitive book in 1954, *Johnny Appleseed: Man and Myth* (Bloomington, Ind.: Indiana University Press).

Florence Murdoch, librarian for the Swedenborg Church in Cincinnati and a descendant of a long and proud line of Swedenborgians, was responsible for creating the New Church Library's important Johnny Appleseed Collection in Cincinnati, Ohio, now housed at Urbana University in Urbana, Ohio. Her poignant concern over how Walt Disney Studios would depict Appleseed's guardian angel in its animated feature *Melody Time* (1948) is articulated in her thoughtful correspondence to Disney, which is included in Urbana's collection. Murdoch also drew the map of Appleseed country found on the end papers of this book.

John W. Stockwell, who contributed an original poem as well as two essays (only one of which is included in the present edition), was a Swedenborgian minister active in promoting New Church insights. He conducted the First Undenominational Radio Church, in which Swedenborgian teachings were applied to social problems, and headed the Group Study Bureau, a New Church adult education program. Stockwell also published several books, among them *Riding the Question Mark through Life Situations and Progress* (1937) and *Swedenborg: Noetic Mystic* (1940).

Ophia D. Smith's important books and articles about early Swedenborgians and New Church history in Ohio are revered by church members. She and her husband, William E. Smith, authored *Buckeye Titan* (Oxford, Ohio: The Oxford Printing Company, 1953), a major biography of John H. James, who founded Urbana University and who married Francis Bailey's daughter, Abigail. Bailey was the first printer in the United States to produce the works of Emanuel Swedenborg.

Since the writings of Emanuel Swedenborg were integral to the philosophy of Johnny Appleseed, it is fitting that the Swedenborg Foundation, under its Chrysalis Books imprint, has reissued this book in its sesquicentennial year of publishing. Having studied John Chapman virtually all my life, I am honored to be associated with this book's original authors, whom I have admired and respected throughout the years. Although they have all passed away, they and the legendary figure about whom they wrote are still very much alive in this book. It is a thoughtful look at how an unassuming man impacted thousands of lives and unwittingly catapulted himself into American folklore merely by "going about doing good."

WILLIAM ELLERY JONES
2000

Johnny Appleseed

A VOICE IN THE WILDERNESS

Johnny Appleseed in American Folklore and Literature

by Robert Price

*A*ny one who wishes to enjoy the true flavor of a Johnny Appleseed tale should first read Henry David Thoreau's pleasant essay on "Wild Apples." Thoreau had apparently never heard of Johnny Appleseed, it is true, and did not include a "Johnny Appleseed Apple" (*Malus appleseediana!*) along with the "Apple that grows in an old Cellar Hole" (*Malus cellaris*), the "Green Apple" (*Malus choleramorbifera, aut dysenterifera, pueriilis dilectissima*), and the rest of the delightful, mythical varieties that he whimsically listed. But he managed to express in his account of these tough seedling apple trees and their pleasantly unpredictable fruit exactly the same rich, untamable qualities that one finds in the myths, folktales, and legends that have sprung up all over the American countryside to perpetuate the name of Johnny Appleseed.

For a number of years, I have been trailing these stories back and forth across the land, staking out facts, mapping the routes the folk beliefs have traveled, and trying to see the whole delightful flock of tales in all their richly interesting historical and imaginary lights. They long ago escaped from man's predictions and governance, I have found. Like most wild things, they are something very rugged and of endless and ever-multiplying variety. They are peculiarly and pleasantly native, always interesting, sometimes unexpectedly rich in flavor, and in their season often very beautiful. Let me tell you something about them.

I

First of all, it should be emphasized that the real John Chapman belongs to true history, and one need have no fear for his reputation when one sets out to untangle the facts from the romances.

In 1817, when John Chapman was forty-two years old, the first known printed account of him, and one of the very few contemporary records, appeared—of all places—in Manchester, England. It was part of a report issued by the Manchester Society for Printing, Publishing, and Circulating the Writings of Emanuel Swedenborg, and had been written by someone in America who apparently had never met or seen John Chapman but who had heard tales of his unusual missionary work, west of the Appalachians [see "Prefatory Notes," Preface 2]. Johnny Appleseed's story would always travel rapidly and far—already in his lifetime, it had gone some thirty-five-hundred miles to make its first appearance on a printed page.

The details of John Chapman's story in this Manchester report were of a decidedly colorful sort, just the kind that would appeal vividly to popular imagination. He was described as an "extraordinary" missionary of the New Jerusalem. He was believed to be devoting the proceeds from his apple nurseries, planted "in numberless places in the wilderness," wholly to the extension of his faith. He was a man of well-nigh supernatural endurance, "almost independent of corporal wants and sufferings." He "had actually thawed the ice with his bare feet." He sometimes divided a book into two or three parts for more extensive distribution. Certain anecdotal bits concerning John Chapman had seemingly already begun to circulate as interesting tales among the mid-westerners who wrote to their friends in the east about him.

We know now, a century and a quarter later, that the basic pattern of this first printed Johnny Appleseed story was the same as that which would appear again and again in various seemingly independent places. Here was the singular personality, the missionary zeal, the seedling nurseries, the primitive existence, the capacity to endure hardships, and certain specific anecdotes to exemplify these traits. Time and again these features of the story would appear, in widely separated neighborhoods of northern Pennsylvania, a dozen counties of Ohio, northern Indiana, and Missouri. Particulars would often be so divergent that one can be almost sure that the tales were of separate origins. But the central story would always be the same.

The reason is that it is grounded in history. No matter how far away from plausibility the fancies go—and at times they have gone very far indeed—one can always feel certain of a nucleus of fact in the career of the historical

John Chapman. Much is even documentable now. We know that Johnny Appleseed was indeed a professional orchardist of a very useful sort; that he was a Swedenborgian missionary; and that he was a hardy, courageous, and undoubtedly eccentric frontiersman. What happened is that all these certifiable facts added up to a personality that somehow managed to set going the creative imaginations of the American common people, first among the folks who knew him, then increasingly in each generation to follow. Today, few Americans are monumentalized by so rich an accumulation of story and reverential belief.

II

Legends expand in typical ways that are as natural as thought itself. Whenever a story such as that of John Chapman begins to germinate in folk imagination, certain developments are always to be expected. First signs of growth usually appear in particular traits of personality or in significant biographical events. If a man has been known for special powers of endurance, folk fancies soon seize upon particular instances of these powers, begin to enhance them into feats of remarkable quality, and then proceed, as the desire for greater color grows, to invent still others that will markedly emphasize the quality admired. Once a life has taken on peculiar significance, creative fancies do not hesitate to decorate all parts of it. Not only the peculiar incidents or traits that first caught attention, but the whole cycle of his birth, youth, education, loves, matting, maturity, and death become significant and grow increasingly in color and particular detail.

Take, for example, what the folk mind has done with the apple symbol in John Chapman's life. Apples very early became a life-symbol in the stories about him. By 1822—when he was forty-eight years old—he was already being called "John Appleseed" by people who knew him in the Midwest, and the symbolical nickname in one variant or another has stuck firmly ever since.[1] For many years, one group of tales has made much of Johnny's supposedly being born in appleblossom time. (He was really born during New England apple-picking, which, considering his interest in apple seeds would have served folk fancies even better.) The appleblossoms, said the tales, even reached down and tapped at the Chapman window the day he arrived. He had no more than opened his tiny blue eyes than he reached up his hands and cried for the beautiful flowers. His youth, they said, was spent in the New England orchards. Much of his inspiration came from these trees. His love was plighted there, and it was beneath the blossoms that the realization came that his love could never be consummated. Years afterward, far out in the Midwest, he planted apple seeds on his sweetheart's grave—planted them to spell the mystic words "apple blossom." When his humanitarian program on the frontier was organized, apples became the central medium of his benevolences. Sometimes, said the stories, he supplied apple seeds in little leather pouches to the pioneers going ahead of him into the wilderness. Others said (and they had a basis of truth) that he was a forerunner of the settlements sowing his seeds and having the young apple trees ready for orchard planting when the settler arrived. He died under the apple trees, of course, with the petals drifting gently down upon him at sunset. (It was really March, a bit early for the apple-blow in Fort Wayne.)

In time, the folk mind gradually made him not only the founder of orchards but of all horticulture in the Midwest. Many important varieties of apples were attributed to his seedlings—Jonathan, Rambo, Baldwin, Clermont, Grimes golden, and many more, though not a single claim can be substantiated. His plantings, according to public claim, extended not merely from western Pennsylvania, over Ohio, into Indiana, as the records would suggest, but from seaboard to seaboard. Recent Federal Writers' Project publications attribute early orchards in Massachusetts and Connecticut to him. Missouri and Arkansas claim him and say that he carried his seeds across the plains to the foothills of the Rockies. A woman once told me in all seriousness that Johnny Appleseed had planted the first orchards in southern California. His name is now honored with equal reverence at apple festivals in Oregon, Virginia, and Vermont. He has become the patron saint of American orchards. Or rather, he has become the mythical planter of all first orchards.

Even more than that, in a recent development, the most interesting and significant of all, Johnny Appleseed and his apple planting have become a symbol of American democracy. John Chapman was the common man, working for the common good. His apple trees were the token of all the unselfish, constructive forces that work in the creation of the true commonwealth. Vachel Lindsay saw the "apple blossom amaranth," which sprang from John Chapman's mystical seeds, enveloping the entire world within a hundred years, and climbing even to the doorstep of heaven.

III

Although Johnny Appleseed's story has had a consistent popular growth from the beginning, several books have been very important at certain times in giving it impulse and direction.

The first of these was a regional history that has been monumental among the local chronicles of the Midwest—Henry Howe's *Historical Collections of Ohio,* published first in 1847. The two-page account of John Chapman that Howe included in his first edition, and that he expanded into four pages in a revision forty-two years later, has been basic to nearly everything of importance written about Johnny Appleseed in later years.

Henry Howe was not a trained historian, and he never had any delusions that he was creating a fact-proof definitive record of the areas which he canvassed. He had set out from New England to make a series of books in the manner of John W. Barber's historical collections of Connecticut (1836) and of Massachusetts (1839), which would combine history, biography, description, and engravings in such a way as to record not only the "present condition and prospects," together with a history of the settlement, of each state he studied, but also "incidents illustrating the customs, the fortitude, the bravery, and the privations of its early settlers" (Preface to first edition, 1847). When Howe arrived at Marietta in 1846 to begin a round-up of these materials in Ohio, he had already published his collections for New York, Pennsylvania, New Jersey, and Virginia. His fullest and most characteristic work, however, was to be done in Ohio. Notebook and sketchbook in hand, he set out early in January 1846 to visit every county, there to converse with old residents, visit graveyards and historic spots, copy original records and manuscripts when available, and make pencil drawings for later woodcuts. In all, he crossed the state four times. He gathered not only facts of history, but anecdotes, personal memoirs, biographies, quaint personality sketches, odds and ends of all sorts so long as they seemed to sample the materials that had gone into the making of this great new West. The resulting volume in 1847 was a varicolored patchwork if there ever were one, but it was a handsome one. Its like had never been produced in the Midwest before. In Ohio, nothing else has ever replaced it. Howe's *Historical Collections of Ohio* has inaccuracies of fact and judgment, we know now, but it remains in spite of all a basic work.

Henry Howe's story of John Chapman was part of this rich gathering. His version came, seemingly, from old residents in that north-central portion of Ohio which centers in Mansfield and Richland County. These Ohioans of 1846 remembered Johnny as a very eccentric character who had frequented that region at an early day. When Howe talked with them, they did not yet know, it appears now, that John Chapman had died the year before near Fort Wayne, Indiana, for Howe did not mention that fact until his revised edition of 1889. They knew only that Chapman had moved on into the far west, they didn't know exactly where, some twenty years before. He had come from New England, they said, had imbibed a remarkable passion for the rearing and cultivation of seedling apple trees, first made his appearance in western Pennsylvania, thence made his way into Ohio, keeping on the outskirts of the settlements and planting his little nurseries in wilderness clearings well ahead of the main tide of settlers, to whom he either sold or gave his young trees, often in exchange for some trifle or a piece of old clothing. He derived self-satisfaction amounting almost to a delight from the indulgence of his engrossing occupation. His personal appearance was singular. He was quick and restless, his hair and beard were long and dark. He lived the roughest life. He went barefooted even in the snow. He was a follower of Swedenborg, leading a blameless life, and likening himself to the primitive Christian taking no thought for the morrow.

This general outline Howe expanded with various local anecdotes. He repeated the story that Chapman tore his Swedenborgian tracts into pieces so that he might share the teachings more widely.[2] Johnny would quench his campfire rather than let it destroy the mosquitoes that flew into its blaze. He once slept on the snow in the open air rather than disturb a mother bear and her cubs in a hollow log that he had selected for his night's lodging. He sighed over his own heartlessness in impulsively killing a rattlesnake that had bitten him.

His clothes also demanded certain specific details. He wore on his head a tin utensil that served both as a cap and a mush pot.[3] His suit consisted mainly of a coffee sack that he wore as a cloak, his head thrusting through a hole in the bottom.

Another story had it that once when an itinerant preacher holding forth on the public square of Mansfield had rhetorically exclaimed, "Where is the bare-footed Christian, traveling to heaven?" Johnny, lying on a pile of lumber nearby had taken the question literally, waved his bare feet in the air and shouted, "Here he is!"[4]

All these anecdotes and descriptive bits probably originated in actual fact. They imply a personality and certain

11

activities that are wholly consistent with those that always appear in earliest local accounts of Johnny Appleseed. But one must not overlook the fact that Howe was recording local traditions that had been passed around for twenty years as a part of normal community story-telling and that had been preserved during that time only in people's memories and imaginations.

Although it is not the function of this paper to relate the documentable history of the real John Chapman, it may be only fair to point out in connection with Howe's account—so important has it been in shaping the popular concept—that other first-hand reports have made no mention of the mush-pot hat or coffeesack dress and suggest normal though ragged clothes; that copies of Swedenborg's *True Christian Religion* printed in Philadelphia were sent west at an early date in unbound form so that the separate foldings or "signatures" (which had never yet seen the covers of a book) could be distributed as tracts; that to leave a mother bear and her cubs undisturbed was the most obvious of common sense; and that John Chapman, though eccentric and zealous in the service of his faith, followed nurserying for nearly fifty years not as an obsession but as a business and, while from modern standpoints not always practical in his methods or blessed with outstanding material success, was never either a fanatical or an indiscriminate dispenser of his substance.

Howe's book was for years the most widely read history in Ohio. Some writers have said it was the most commonly read book outside the Bible. Howe may not have written definitive history, doing too much of what G. K. Chesterton once called "tail-end journalistic reporting"— that is, taking the current final beliefs about things rather than probing thoroughly to their sources. But he caught something that was vital and vigorous just the same. He gave the sons and grandsons of the frontier a background of fact and tradition to be proud of. And in the case of Johnny Appleseed, although his account was very possibly colored by a particular community's accumulated lore, there is abundant evidence now from other sources that the fancies did not replace but only enhanced the original personality and life.

Howe's story was not only read, it was variously reprinted. The *New Church Repository* of August 1852, for example, retold it almost intact. In addition, Howe inspired other similar and increasingly detailed accounts. The period from 1850 to 1890 was the era of county history writing in Ohio. Every neighborhood was gathering the scattered evidences of its immediate past from records, from memories of old residents, and often, when facts failed, out of imagination. Many Midwestern communities had known Johnny Appleseed, or liked to claim that they had, and Howe's volume furnished the necessary prompting to record the claim. These histories have helped preserve many important biographical facts about John Chapman; they also have given credence to numerous fancies.

Johnny Appleseed had also soon become a theme for creative writers; and although the novelists and poets have always used him with honest fictional intent, the uncritical reader has not always been careful to note which parts of historically based stories are documentable and which are only figment. The first of these novels appeared in 1858. *Philip Seymour, or Pioneer Life in Richland County, Ohio* by Reverend James F. M'Gaw of Mansfield used Johnny as a subordinate figure in a thin Cooperesque plot based upon the Copus Indian massacre in his county during the War of 1812. For the most part, M'Gaw followed Howe closely—at times verbatim. But three of the additions in the story (probably based upon previously unrecorded local stories) have since broken away from *Philip Seymour* and have grown vigorously as separate episodes in the Appleseed saga.

M'Gaw recorded that John Chapman, an earnest Swedenborgian, who never married, claimed to have had visions of two wives who would share his life in the afterworld. Since the notion of two spouses is not orthodox Swedenborgianism, one must conclude that whatever visions of conjugal love Chapman may have related, the details got badly distorted in the telling. It has been retold many times, sometimes with humor bordering upon the ribald, sometimes as in Vachel Lindsay's poetry with consummate beauty.

M'Gaw also made John Chapman a participant in the events of the Copus massacre, although it was not until years later that local chroniclers began to think up a detailed account of his heroic role, part of which, they claimed, was to run the twenty miles from Mansfield to the blockhouse in Mount Vernon for assistance.[5] In still later versions, Johnny Appleseed has become the man who at that time really saved all the frontier settlements from the Indian ravages that threatened during the opening months of the war with Britain.

A third contribution of the *Philip Seymour* story was an honestly fictitious account of Johnny's death scene, idyllic, peaceful, with readings from the Beatitudes under the trees at the close of a beautiful summer day. The description soon became a part of standard biographical sketches which have been widely reprinted even to the present day.

In the November 1871 issue of *Harper's New Monthly Magazine,* there appeared an article by W. D. Haley entitled "Johnny Appleseed: A Pioneer Hero," which in some ways has been the most influential piece of all about John Chapman.[6] Professor B. A. Botkin has very rightfully used it in his recent *Treasury of American Folklore* (1944) to represent the entire Johnny Appleseed saga, for the *Harper's* article lifted Johnny's story out of the American Midwest and spread it across the land. Furthermore, it did so with such appeal and conviction that traces of Haley's interpretation can be found in almost all later writing on the subject, especially that of a literary sort. Haley built upon Howe, repeating the same anecdotes, adding many more, and very definitely intensifying each traditional aspect of Johnny's character and life history as it had been established earlier.

Haley was from the same central Ohio region that had given Howe's version. He gathered his new material, he said, chiefly from "the memories of old residents who remembered Johnny." He added details concerning Johnny's eccentricities of habits and dress. Johnny's humanitarianism, previously associated with bears, mosquitoes, and snakes, was now extended to hornets and horses. His kindly deeds to his fellow men were many and tenderly remembered. His missionary activities had taken on drama and beauty. One woman recalled his reading—"his voice rising denunciatory and thrilling—strong and loud as the roar of wind and waves, then soft and soothing as the balmy airs that quivered the morning-glory leaves about his gray beard." There was a hint of an early disappointment in love. One of Haley's informants recalled that Johnny's role in the War of 1812 (fifty-nine years before) had really been a very brilliant one and even quoted his precise words that bright moonlit night as he ran from cabin to cabin warning the settlers of an impending massacre: "The spirit of the Lord is upon me, and he hath anointed me to blow the trumpet in the wilderness, and sound an alarm in the forest; for, behold, the tribes of the heathen are round about your doors, and a devouring flame followeth after them." Haley gave many more details; I have picked out only a few that have made particularly strong appeals to later imaginations.

Much of Haley's data seems to have come from Rosella Rice of this same central Ohio region, whose recollections had been quoted in H. S. Knapp's *History of Ashland County, Ohio* in 1863. Miss Rice was a local fiction writer whose novel *Mabel* (1857) and many shorter contributions to T. S. Arthur's *Illustrated Home Magazine, Godey's Lady's Book,* and other women's journals were of the conventionally sentimental quality that has caused one decade in American writing to be called appropriately the "Feminine Fifties." Rice claimed that her account of Johnny was based chiefly upon recollections. As a matter of fact, Rice was born at approximately the time when Chapman is known to have left central Ohio for northern Indiana. She must have remembered him only from his later occasional trips to his old Ohio haunts, the last of which may have occurred when she was approximately twelve years old. Her story of Johnny was vivid, dramatic, and lush with feeling, the normal product of a very active and romantically inclined imagination. For years she continued to enlarge and intensify this story of Johnny in various contributions to local papers and histories. It is her only work for which she is remembered now. One version appeared in the second edition of *Philip Seymour* (1883) and was copied by Howe in his second edition of 1889. Henry Howe, W. D. Haley, and Rosella Rice, although they undoubtedly passed along to later generations a large body of very precious fact, also set the directions for romantic imaginations. The accounts of all three writers were reprinted and embroidered over and over for many years in local histories and horticultural reports throughout the Middle West, and in newspapers and magazines all over the country. One still runs into them as regularly as September or May comes around.

IV

To trace all the accumulations around Johnny Appleseed's story through the years would be tedious and perhaps no more fruitful than some of those wild seedling apple trees that perpetuate his name. Let me pick out a few of the more important developments here and there.

Many charming stories flock around John Chapman's youth. In Springfield, Massachusetts, an idyll of considerable proportions has developed. The boy growing up in a cabin there with a beautiful apple tree in the yard overlooking the Connecticut River was mission-touched from the first. What hours he could spend away from his books and the orchards seem to have been devoted to the forests where the wild creatures flocked around him, as around St. Francis of old, to hear him talk and read.

The seeds planted by the earlier chroniclers in their half-hints of an unfulfilled love blossomed gloriously at the beginning of the twentieth century. The Reverend Newell Dwight Hillis's novel *The Quest of John Chapman* (1904) was the first to develop a full narrative, and the formula he used has stuck ever since. John Chapman in this very sentimentally romantic story was the son of a Massachusetts divine and was a student at Harvard. He loved Dorothy Durand, daughter of his father's bitterest enemy in the congregation, but the parents' hostility prevented their marriage. The Durands moved west with a company going to Ohio and were eventually swallowed up in the strange lands beyond the mountains. John conceived the seed-planting mission as a device for searching out his lost sweetheart. He found her at last in Kentucky, but too late. She had died only a short time before of a strange fever and a broken heart. Thereafter, John's orcharding became sublimated into a life mission of humanitarian service. Nearly fifty years after Dorothy Durand's death, the aged Johnny Appleseed returned to her grave to plant there the apple seeds which sprouted the following June to spell symbolic words.

This is a very obviously conventional plot. I have summarized it only because of its effects upon the later legend. Although Reverend Hillis invented the love story and practically all the other episodic material in his book, the story had just enough foundation in fact for uncritical readers too let much of it slip easily into popular acceptance. The Harvard scholar invention has stuck firmly. It even appears in a current biography with the statement that John Chapman was the brightest scholar in the class—Harvard librarians have been pestered for years with inquiries concerning his nonexistent record. The unrequited love theme has remained pretty well as Hillis left it. Sometimes the young woman's name is Sara Crawford or Betty Stacey, or something else, but the long separation of the lovers and the death of the maiden just when they are about to be united are now firmly fixed in the legend.[7] Whole episodes from Hillis's novel have been retold as history. I have found the love plot solemnly recorded in the publication of two

Midwestern historical societies, and the current book-length biography even relates the story of the old man's visit to the Kentucky grave and the seeds that sprouted into "Apple Blossom."

Two other novels have added interesting episodes to the saga. That very popular romancer of the nineties, Mary Hartwell Catherwood, made the trail of Johnny Appleseed cross that of the "Lost Dauphin," the story-crowned son of Louis XVI and Marie Antoinette, whose supposed escape from France intrigued the imaginations of a whole generation of American readers. An incident in Catherwood's best-selling thriller *Lazarre* (1902), in which Johnny gave valued assistance to the exiled prince, seems to have passed over at once into accepted history. One finds interesting reflections of it in such recent publications as Louis Bromfield's *The Farm* and Harlan Hatcher's *The Buckeye Country.*

In 1915, Eleanor Atkinson published her pleasant little novel *Johnny Appleseed: The Romance of the Sower,* which has had many readers ever since. This book has added much to recent popular belief. One episode, wholly original with Atkinson, has been especially important. Atkinson, who has been amazed at the facility with which her sincerely fictional material has been taken over into folk history, began her story with a vivid account of a Johnny Appleseed nursery and orchard at Pittsburgh in 1799. This was, in the story, Johnny's initial undertaking in the west. Here, at the gateway to the Ohio country, he was providing young trees or little buckskin sacks of apple seeds for the settlers going on ahead of him into the wilderness. At the same time from his Pittsburgh orchard and from other resources, he was furnishing the weary travelers past his door with food and other kindly aids. Atkinson wrote me twenty-two years later that she had created the Pittsburgh nursery and traveler's aid station out of two known facts: there was an old orchard, of unknown origin, at a very early day on Grant's Hill above the town; and Johnny had been credited in central Ohio traditions with having been in the Allegheny Valley. Atkinson's Pittsburgh episode in the story was accepted at once as real history and has since been supplemented with many specific details—names of people who knew him, taverns he visited, even the Conestoga wagon on which he made his triumphal entry in Pittsburgh, and specific instances of the buckskin bag gifts of apple seeds. No evidence that John Chapman actually lived in Pittsburgh, however, has ever come to light. In fact, much fact points definitely to the contrary, although he could have visited the town, inasmuch as he was working in the Allegheny Valley in the period from 1797 to 1804 and possibly later.

Another episode that has grown so imperceptibly that it is difficult to place the credit for specific creation concerns John Chapman's heroic adventures as a wilderness scout and mediary between the whites and Indians. That he knew the primeval trails, was on friendly relations with the Indians, and was present on the frontier in Ohio during some of the blood-spilling in the War of 1812 are all seemingly authenticable facts. We have noted already the growth of his reputation as a savior of the border settlements. It was inevitable that his name would become associated sooner or later with General William Henry Harrison, the popular hero of those troubled years, and with his most notable battle. The episode is a very recent addition to the Appleseed tales, but it is already firmly established. The current biography of John Chapman expands it into an eight-page account and makes Johnny Appleseed the man who really saved the day for Harrison's militia at Tippecanoe.[8]

This tendency to pick up friends among the great is always characteristic of a folk hero. According to the biography just mentioned, Johnny Appleseed served not only under General Harrison, but also under General George Rogers Clark and General Anthony Wayne; he was well acquainted with all the famous scouts of his time including Daniel Boone, Simon Kenton, and the Wetzels; he was on friendly relations also with John James Audubon and with Abraham Lincoln. There is, of course, no more support for these claims than for the one recorded in Missouri that he fought in the battle of Lookout Mountain (twenty years after his death). More plausible is the scene in Henry Bailey Stevens' delightful play of American folklore in which Johnny Appleseed strives against no less an antagonist than the great, destructive Paul Bunyon himself to preserve the soul of the American forests.

When all that is obvious myth in the story of John Chapman is set against everything that is certain fact, it becomes increasingly evident that, while he was undoubtedly a historical personage of worthy stature, he was also in nearly every way a much simpler man than the folk fancies would make him. He was much less grotesque, probably had only relatively few of the adventures now ascribed to him, was less abnormal in thought and habit than the tales would make out, and lived generally much closer to the rugged pattern demanded by normal frontier necessity than a later generation has preferred to believe. People loved him and remembered him just as much because he was one of them as because he was singularly apart from them.

V

The poets and story makers have labored long and well to catch the elusive something behind the historic personage.

I have already mentioned various novels that have become inescapably enmeshed by now in the intricacies of the saga. Other fictional uses of Johnny Appleseed in either major or minor capacity can be found in Merle Colby's *All Ye People,* Howard Fast's *The Tall Hunter,* Robert Harper's *Trumpet in the Wilderness,* Clark McMeekin's *Recon with the River,* Ethel Hull Miller's *Out of the Roaring Loom,* Mary Schumann's *My Blood and My Treasure,* Denton J. Snider's *The Freeburgers,* and—most significant of all—Vachel Lindsay's *The Golden Book of Springfield,* to be discussed shortly.

The playwrights have done nearly as well as the novelists. Johnny has appeared in many a piece, on both the adult and juvenile levels. He pops up regularly in radio scripts. He is so obviously the very stuff of pageantry that Midwestern dramatizations of local history are rarely without him. The finest tribute of the stage so far, however, is probably Marc Connelly's and Arnold Sundgaard's *Everywhere I Roam,* which opened for a short run at the National Theatre, New York, on December 29, 1938. In it, Johnny became a symbol of all the wholesomeness that centers in the land and in simple living as opposed to the standardizing and eventually destructive forces arising from modern industrialism.

It is the poets, though, who have carried Johnny Appleseed's theme into the highest reaches of imaginative interpretation. For the poet, as Emerson once pointed out, is free of "authors and the public and heeds only this one dream that holds him like an insanity." The poet's work is worth more, therefore, than all the scholars' "arguments and histories and criticism." He or she is free and makes free. The poet's true function is to find the essential truth behind the particular thing or event or personality. It matters not whether Johnny Appleseed planted Fall Pippins or Ben Davises—the fruit the poet garners is of vastly richer quality. Of the many fine poems that have been published, let me pick out a few which carry special import.

The first was Lydia Maria Child's "Apple-Seed John." Bibliographers still puzzle over just when it was first published; but when Child died in 1880 at the age of seventy-eight, it was already in circulation and has since been the most frequently reprinted of all the Appleseed poems—probably the best known bit today of Child's voluminous writings. The poem relates in simple ballad style the early version of the kindly nurseryman that we have seen chronicled in the 1840s and 1850s. It does not overemphasize mushpot hats or visions, unrequited love, heroism, or superhuman endurance, but tells a quiet story of a kindly, unspectacular man who found his peculiar way to do some good in the world. Perhaps the naturalness of the telling has given the verses their long appeal. Child's concept of Johnny must have come from the decades before 1850, when the Appleseed story was first having its extension in its earlier simple form. She may have heard it first through Swedenborgian publications, which she read earnestly for many years. The last three of her twenty-one stanzas suggest the quiet dignity of the whole:

> So he kept on traveling far and wide,
> Till his old limbs failed him, and he died.
> He said at the last: "Tis a comfort to feel
> I've done good in the world, though not a great deal."

Weary travelers, journeying west,

In the shade of his trees find pleasant rest;

And they often start, with glad surprise,

At the rosy fruit that round them lies.

And if they inquire whence came such trees,

Where not a bough once swayed in the breeze,

The answer still comes, as they travel on:

"These trees were planted by Apple-Seed John."

In 1894, the most curious of all Appleseed verse appeared in *Johnny Appleseed's Rhymes* published in St. Louis by Denton J. Snider ("Theophilus Middling"). In the novel *The Freeburgers*, published five years earlier, Snider had introduced Johnny as an old itinerant fiddler who, in addition to his regular seed planting went about playing tunes and making up rhymes and songs to fit all occasions. His fiddle, somewhat larger than ordinary, he played in several ways. "He would thrum it, or pick it, like a guitar; he would place it between his knees like a violoncello, and draw the bow upon its strings; finally he would put it against his shoulder and play it like the ordinary violin." He sang with a voice "of finest texture." Few heroes have possessed the versatility of Johnny Appleseed. It is not surprising, accordingly, to find him appearing in Snider's next book as a peripatetic minstrel and philosopher, in addition to his usual role as seedman. He had been in Ohio, Indiana, Kentucky, Tennessee, Illinois, and as far west as the Rockies, and had fought in the Civil War, although he never formally enlisted. His customary procedure when he visited a community was to go to the public square and there begin to play and sing.

The country people would gather around to listen while he gave forth in such aphoristic jingles as the following:

> Seize the present occasion
> Make the poem to fit:
> Today is the whole of creation,
> Hath the eternal in it.

*   *   *   *   *   *   *   *

> Even to the mule
> Man can sometimes go to school
> If the man too be a mule.

*   *   *   *   *   *   *   *

> Because it fits so snugly
> The shoe is so ugly.

This poetical, philosophical Johnny had, in fact, read all the German philosophers and could even discourse on Darwin. His rhymes are presented with running comment by the author in the manner of Carlyle's *Sartor Resartus*. There is a melange of pseudoscholarship, comparison of versions, references to ancients and moderns, and philological flitter-flutter. Denton J. Snider, a St. Louis Hegelian, was among those who lectured in Bronson Alcott's School of Philosophy in Concord. In these rhymes of Snider, Johnny Appleseed wandered closer than in any other work to the Emersonian center of philosophical idealism that marked his era.

Perhaps Snider's books were responsible for a late trans-Mississippi extension of the Appleseed myth in which

Johnny has indeed become a wandering fiddler as well as orchardist. Such a development is clearly shown in the folk version given in Fred W. Alsopp's *Folklore of Romantic Arkansas* (1931). Perhaps his shade is merging there with that of the Arkansas Traveler, just as in Missouri, according to one writer, it has merged with a ribald Johnny Applejack, and as in Pennsylvania I have found it in recent years becoming confused with an historic Coal Oil Johnny from the Allegheny oil country.

Carl Sandburg, Edgar Lee Masters, Francis Frost, Stephen Vincent and Rosemary Benét, and Vachel Lindsay have all contributed short poetical tributes in later years—to mention from the many only a few whose names have national currency.

My favorite of these shorter works, I think, is the trim little ballad, "Johnny Appleseed" which the Benéts put into their *Book of Americans* (1933). It is a folksy piece, unpretentious but perfectly turned, quite worthy of a better adornment than the ugly cartoon which the illustrator of the volume gave it. The ballad has caught on in public approval and is already being sung to a setting by Elie Siegmeister.

The longest and the finest poetical tribute to Johnny Appleseed has come from Vachel Lindsay. Lindsay had grown up in the country of the Appleseed tales. Later, when as a poet he set out to find a native theme through which he could depict what he wished more than anything else to express, the soul of America and its salvation, he found himself returning again and again, after many experiments with other historical and legendary materials, to the story of John Chapman. "He was the New England kind of saint," Lindsay explained in *The Litany of Washington Street* (1929), "much like a Hindu saint, akin to Thoreau and Emerson. . . . He kept moving for a lifetime toward the sunset, on what we would call 'The Mystical Johnny Appleseed Highway,' leaving in his wake orchards bursting and foaming with rich fruit, gifts for mankind to find long after. . . . Johnny Appleseed's apple trees marched straight west, past his grave at Fort Wayne, Indiana, through the best apple country of Illinois to the Pacific, and stand there singing Whitman's 'Passage to India.'"

As early as 1920, in his extraordinary and chaotically beautiful novel *The Golden Book of Springfield,* Lindsay had already developed quite elaborately this idea of John Chapman as a symbol of the redeeming forces in American democracy. In this strange book, Johnny became by the year 2018 a canonized saint. Certain seeds that he had once given in an old leather seed-sack to a companion traveler in the forests and that had been planted in Sangamon County, Illinois, had produced the world's first orchards of the "Apple Amaranth," a mystic fruit that engendered heroes and imparted to all who partook of it a love of eternal beauty. Pilgrims followed the old Johnny Appleseed highways eastward and westward to plant not only America but all the world with the sacred groves of Amaranth. In time, the boughs mounted even to the walls of heaven where they clambered over to adorn the highest towers.

In 1921, Lindsay published in *The Spectator* a long poem entitled "Song for American Children in Praise of Johnny Appleseed." The work was rambling and uneven, but it contained some of the most beautiful lines Lindsay had yet written. The poem expressed his usual idealism, embodying it in a rugged, vivid account of Johnny's career from his crossing the eastern mountains to his death at

Forth Wayne. Later, Lindsay condensed and revised this work for his *Collected Poems* and is said to have called it the poem in which he took the greatest personal pride.

Lindsay never dropped the Appleseed theme. Lyric after lyric came to his mind, which I am inclined to feel he intended at some later time to incorporate into one long work. Sometimes it was John Chapman's mystic love episodes, as in the beautiful "Johnny Appleseed's Wife of the Mind." Again, it was a sacred song as in "Johnny Appleseed's Hymn to the Sun" or a vision of the future America, "Johnny Appleseed Speaks of the Appleblossom Amaranth That Will Come to This City," "Johnny Appleseed's Ship Comes In," or "How Johnny Appleseed Walked Alone in the Jungle of Heaven."

In two beautiful fragments published in 1923, the poet had glimpses of the mystical Johnny in the far west on the mountain peak called "Going-to-the-Sun." The phantom orchardist was eating an apple from which, when he idly threw away the core, other apples instantly went rolling down the green mountainside. "And fairies came from them." In the other glimpse, old Johnny just at sunset was at prayer. Suddenly, the sun became Johnny Appleseed's great apple barrel, the hoops of which broke asunder and sent dark rich apples rolling down the world—

> red and russet domes
> That turned to clouds of glory and strange homes
> Above the mountaintops for cloud-born souls:—
> Reproofs for men, if they would build the world
> As Johnny Appleseed would have it done.

Lindsay never quite succeeded in accomplishing the perfect poetical integration he long sought, either to express the soul of America or to tell the story of Johnny Appleseed. Most of his various Appleseed lyrics he brought together in the opening pages of the 1927 edition of his *Collected Poems.* By that time, he had reached the period of his short life when he was unable to carry out the sustained creative effort he most desired. Yet, as late as 1929, he was still eagerly collecting information about John Chapman, seemingly in preparation for further work.

Better than he realized, perhaps, all his short poems on Johnny Appleseed really do fit into a general pattern and can be read today as one long work of great dignity and power. The most finished portion of it—the long "In Praise of Johnny Appleseed"—has been given a beautiful choral setting by Eunice Lea Kettering.

John Chapman died, so it is said, on March 18, 1845, in the cabin of William Worth of St. Joseph's Township, Allen County, Indiana. Perhaps it is peculiarly appropriate a hundred years later that local historians of Fort Wayne cannot completely agree as to where the seventy-year-old man was buried. Somehow one gets the feeling sooner or later that the true Johnny Appleseed is something quite apart from either birth or death.

Certainly there is an abundance of evidence that some part of him is still very energetically alive. In the autumn of 1942, residents of Noble and Washington counties, Ohio, like those of various other communities erected a monument to John Chapman's memory below Dexter City in the Duck Creek valley where John Chapman's father and family once lived. The monument was placed along the highway at the foot of a hill on the brow of which is an old cemetery containing the graves of Johnny's half-brother and other members of the family. There are also several very old apple trees there.

The following autumn, says a news report that has come in even as these paragraphs were being drafted, a small boy on his way one morning to gather nuts was astounded to see a gray-bearded, twinkling-eyed old man, barefooted, mushpot on head, poised on an apple bough up in the old cemetery. The stranger was munching an apple and reading a tract of Swedenborg. Shortly afterward, a mailman going to deliver to a mother a letter from her soldier son overseas was surprised by the same apparition. And a little later, a woman on her way to help a sick neighbor also saw it. The three separate and impartial observations must be accepted as incontrovertible corroboration. Johnny Appleseed indeed remains very much alive.

Editor's Update

1. An important afterthought on a long-forgotten store ledger from 1816 was discovered in the 1980s by two genealogists, Mary Jane Henney and Maxine Kinton. While researching unrelated data at the Ohio Historical Society library in Columbus, Ohio, they discovered in the account book of Sturges & Sherwood, the following entry on page 100, dated May 18, 1816: "John Chapman or as some say Appleseed" for "2 plugs tobacco $1.00." (Years later, Rosella Rice remarked that John "was a constant snuff user.") Whether the tobacco was intended for someone else is unknown. This entry now is the earliest reference to his sobriquet. The six-year difference from the 1822 date cited by Price is significant as it proves that John's persona was known and revered with affection at least by the end of the War of 1812. Once again,

history is not changed; rather, it is enhanced by the knowledge that John was so warmly regarded at such an early date.

2. Early Swedenborg tracts were printed in octavo of six or seven sections, comprising a total of forty-eight or fifty-six pages. The blue-paper-covered tracts were stitched together with string in three places and easily "separated" into individual sections. Surely, John Chapman was careful not to "tear" pages from the tracts.

3. A few pioneers' reminiscences do report seeing Chapman with a "tin case" of some sort being worn upon his head. These references are products from his later years. Perhaps, if he was loaded down with other provisions, he did indeed use the utensil in this innovative manner. Tin was light and thin and could be molded easily to the contour of one's skull, but one wonders about its practicality under hot sun or hail storms!

4. The barefooted Christian episode transpired in Mansfield Square in 1827. The pile of lumber upon which John Chapman reclined was reserved for construction of the city's new court house that same year.

5. Although the details of Chapman's participation in the Copus massacre are unclear, countless Ohio county histories perpetuate his involvement. A surviving son of the incident, Wesley Copus, was quoted in 1878 as saying, "Chapman acquitted himself with distinction."

6. W. D. Haley was a newspaper man who, during the winter of 1870–1871, worked on the *Loudonville Independent*, Loudonville, Ohio. His *Harper's* article also was republished in the *Ashland Times* (Ohio), on Thursday, November 9, 1871.

7. In 1943, a correspondent from Willimantic, Connecticut, wrote to Anna Long Onstott, "Alice Rudd was his [Chapman's] fiancee. She was to go to him in Pennsylvania, but did not go." John's older sister, Elizabeth, married Nathaniel Rudd of Charlemont in the Commonwealth of Massachusetts, December 1799.

8. Price is referencing Henry Pershing's book *Johnny Appleseed and His Time* (Strasburg, Va.: Shenandoah Publishing House, Inc., 1930). Mainly a work of fiction, it did include some facts and a few rare photographs.

The Arts Salute
Johnny Appleseed

by Florence Murdoch

Sensing the beauty and significance of the selfless, useful life of the pioneer planter extraordinary "Johnny Appleseed" (John Chapman) and recognizing the picturesque quality of his frontier surroundings, poets have vied with fiction writers and dramatists in limning a composite word-portrait of this strangely interesting character and his unique combination of temporal and spiritual pursuits.

Selections have been made for this anthology from more than thirty poems, rhymes, and ballads. Of course, the originals should be read in their entirety to catch the full flavor. These verses have appeared scattered through such diverse publications as children's and young people's magazines, agricultural journals and historical books, magazines and pamphlets, in poetry anthologies and in musical settings, as well as in newspapers. A number of poems are still unpublished, and the end is not yet; for the theme seems perennial and capable of infinite variation.

How vivid is this personal description in the poem "Johnny Appleseed" by Florence Boyce Davis:

Who comes there with a leathern sack
Bulging over his homespun back,
Barefoot, hatless, alert and slim—
What is the mission that calls to him?
His queer gray frock is thin and worn,
Stretched in service and bramble-torn,
But he goes his way over the native fox
Under the tangle, over the rocks,
And his eyes with gentle fervor glow
Like the soft, wild eyes of the mountain doe.

John Chapman's "forty years in the wilderness" and his labor of love as a nurseryman are told and retold in varied and charming lines. One of the oldest poems contains these verses touching his problem, his plan, and his work:

Poor Johnny was bended well-nigh double
With years of toil, and care, and trouble;
But his large old heart still felt the need
Of doing for others some kindly deed . . .

Old Johnny said: . . . .
"There's a way for me!"

He worked, and he worked with might and main,
But no one knew the plan in his brain.
He took ripe apples in pay for chores,
And carefully cut from them all the cores.

He filled a bag full then wandered away,
And no man saw him for many a day. . . .

With pointed cane deep holes he would bore,
And in every hole he placed a core;
Then covered them well, and left them there
In keeping of sunshine, rain and air. . . .

And so, as time passed and he traveled on,
Everyone called him "Old Apple-Seed John.". . .

From *Appleseed John* by Lydia Maria Child.

—— 🌳 ——

And here is one that claims to be oldest of all:

> There's a hero worth the singing that no poet's lips have
> sung,
> A prophet of the wilderness whose deeds have found no
> tongue,
> A homely, humble-hearted man—a gentle spirit sent
> To cheer the world and plant the newer gospel as he
> went—
> A specter of the solitudes, whose bare feet, where they
> pressed,
> Prankt with never-dying beauty the dark borders of the
> West—
> A druid of the valley, but as wordless as the wave,
> Scorning comfort—seeking nothing for the good things
> that he gave—
> A poor old plodding pilgrim of a brave, unselfish breed,
> God showed the way and shod the feet of Johnny
> Appleseed. . . .
>
> A song for Johnny Appleseed, who left a living trail
> Of beauty everywhere he went, in mountain or in vale;
> Through many a vanished summer sang the birds and
> hummed the bees
> Amid the bending blossoms of his broad old apple trees,
> Before the tardy vanguard of the foremost pioneers,
> Came to pluck the welcome fruitage in that wilderness of
> theirs;

A health to Johnny Appleseed! And may his glory be
Regrafted in the years to come on Life's eternal tree,
And as long as poor humanity stands naked in its need,
God send us souls as white as that of Johnny Appleseed.

From an article in the
Cincinnati Commercial Gazette, August 8, 1891
"Dedicated to the American Horticultural Society"

——— 🌳 ———

Here are variations on the theme from different poets:

Behind him lay the settlements,
Before him lay a plan
To make the earth a better place
For every fellow man. . . .

Day by day, in the untamed wood,
In a space by the river reeds,
He cleared the land for a nursery,
And planted his apple seeds.

Night by night, at a settler's fire,
On a cabin floor of earth,
He told the old, old story,
Of the Savior's manger birth. . . .

John Chapman's apple trees produced
Their rosy fruit and fair;

John Chapman's scattered Bible leaves
Proclaimed the Lord was there.

Oh green above was the forest roof,
And green below, the sod,
When Chapman walked the wilderness
In company with God.

From *The Ballad of John Chapman*
by Benjamin Wallace Douglass

——— 🌳 ———

Of Jonathan Chapman
Two things are known
That he loved apples,
That he walked alone.

At seventy-odd
He was gnarled as could be,
But ruddy and sound
As a good apple tree.

For fifty years over
Of harvest and dew,
He planted his apples
Where no apples grew.
The winds of the prairie

Might blow through his rags,
But he carried his seeds
In the best deerskin bags.

From old Ashtabula
To frontier Fort Wayne,
He planted and pruned
And he planted again. . . .

He nested with owl,
And with bear cub and 'possum,
And knew all his orchards
Root, tendril, and blossom.

The stalking Indian,
The beast in its lair
Did no hurt
While he was there.

For they could tell,
As wild things can,
That Jonathan Chapman
Was God's own man. . . .

From Rosemary and Stephen Vincent Benét,
A Book of Americans (1933)
Set to music by Elie Siegmaster

A typical visit to a pioneer family is mirrored in dialogue
form:

>"What will you take for a strong young tree?
>Times are mighty hard, as you can see,
>But I can't miss a chance such as this seems to be,
>>Johnny Appleseed.". . .

>>"A five-penny bit, or an old shirt, or a shoe
>>or two, neighbor.". . .

>"What do you carry in your pocket today
>To show a little girl? For I have heard say
>They always hope you'll be coming their way,
>>Johnny Appleseed.
>What is it hanging out this side?
>And isn't that new calico you're trying to hide?
>What do you carry in your pocket, Appleseed Johnny?"

>"Patches for your quilt, sister, and a ribbon for your
>hair." . . .

>"How shall I make that dog-fennel tea,
>When chills and fever lay hold of me?
>And have you any catnip, Appleseed Johnny?"

>"Plant this seed by a wet moon, Granny."

>"What is that book you hold in your hand?
>We see few books in this wild land.

Are the words in it very hard to understand,
    Johnny Appleseed?". . .

"A message straight from heaven, neighbor.
Hand me my kit for a rest to my head
    Here by the fire.
Throw on another chunk, and then
List you to the word of God;
For he says to you, and you, and you, little sister,
'Blessed are the pure in heart,
For they shall see God.' "

From *Johnny Appleseed Comes*
by Elizabeth Peck

——— 🌳 ———

Gastronomic possibilities are not overlooked by poets, if one may judge by these mouth-watering excerpts:

Long ago on a fine spring day
Johnny Appleseed came this way
And over hill and meadowland
Scattered his seeds with lavish hand
Here are Jonathan, Bellflower, Northern Spy,
Apples for baking, apples for pie,
Rhode Island Greening, Maidenblush,
Winesap, Pippin, McIntosh,

Russet, Ben Davis, Grimes Yellow Gold,
Rambo and Baldwin to store in the cold,
Rich apple butter and cider for all,
Transparent jelly from apples that fall.
Apples are gathered in orchards today
For Johnny Appleseed came this way.

Johnny Appleseed Came This Way
by Mary Ferguson Legler.

———— 🌳 ————

Johnny, Johnny Appleseed,
What a funny man, indeed!
Not a thing, day in, day out,
Johnny ever thought about,
Only apples. Early, late,
Apples peeled and apples ate,
Apples planted without fail
Up the hill and down the dale,
Till the people, all agreed,
Named him Johnny Appleseed.

Up and down the land he went,
Apple-ing to heart's content,
Year by year, enjoyment found
Planting apple trees around.
Till at last, when spring began,
People cried, "Why, bless the man!"

Here and there, and high and low,
Apple blooms began to blow,
Pearly pink and ivory white,
Shining in the morning light;
Soon some little dingy plot
Shining like a beauty spot!

Then when autumn came, there'd be
Richness shaken from each tree:
Pippins, winesaps, russets brown,
Summer sweetings tumbling down,
Apples, apples everywhere.
Housewives gathered them with care;
Stewed them, baked them,
Boiled them, fried them,
Apple-puffed and apple-pied them,
Cooked them well for every need,

* * * * * * * *

Thank you, Johnny Appleseed!

From *Rhyme of Johnny Appleseed*
by Nancy Byrd Turner

—— 🌳 ——

Apple-blossoms are garlanded about the legendary love-theme, in the minds of many poets:

"A wife and a babe and an apple tree,"
    Jonathan Chapman cried,
"Are the finest things that a man can see!"
    Then—Jonathan's sweetheart died.

Jonathan's loss, the neighbors thought,
    And some of them plainly said,
Turned him more than a sane man ought
    To the third of the three, instead.

* * * *

A wife and a babe with small, pink toes—
    These would have filled his world.
Instead, his children were only rows
    Of apple bloom, tight-curled,

Of orchards waiting some other's wife,
    Of fruit for another's son.
And so he lived his long, strange life
    Though his story is never done

While apple trees lift arms to greet
    The day—and drop, like snow,
Their petals where young lovers meet
    Or tiny children go.

From *Johnny Appleseed Song*
by Virginia Scott Miner

44

Johnny Appleseed speaks:

"She kissed me when the year was young:
    Ah, tender little first caress,
As shy as robin's unlearned song,
    As sweet with wistful happiness!

"All gracious was the season then,
    The air was laden with perfume
And tremulous with music when
    We kissed beneath the apple-bloom.

"Her eyes the summer heaven did hold,
    And drifting petals touched her hair;
But hardly was the year grown old
    Till drifting snows had shrouded her.

* * * *

        . . . The wilderness
Shall blossom in thy memory.
        A host unseen thy name shall bless."

From *Blossoms in the Wilderness*
by Elizabeth R. Kellogg

——— 🌳 ———

Did you know that there were fairies in the Ohio Country?
If there were, Johnny surely knew them! At any rate, a poet
hears them sing at nightfall to the little people of the forest.

45

The Fairies Song

Come, sprite and elf and gnome, draw near,
Our comrade now is dreaming;
We'll whisper words of love and cheer,
And thoughts of gentle seeming.
Go tell the hawk and loon and owl
Their night watch to be keeping;
Go tell the wolf to cease his howl,
The friend of all is sleeping.

When morning comes, the birds of air,
Rejoice when they have found him;
And little creatures gather there,
In perfect trust around him.
He speaks a tongue all nature knows,
In field and woodland bower,
To all that lives to all that grows,
To beast and bird and flower.

Unseen Chorus of Fairies

Peace and love attend you, gentle comrade;
God above defend you, gentle comrade;
All along your kindly way,
We shall guide you day by day,

Dreams of beauty send you, gentle comrade,
So farewell!

> From *Johnny Appleseed,* an operetta for children
> Libretto by David Stevens
> Music by Harvey Worthington Loomis

Johnny Appleseed was a favorite figure with Vachel Lindsay. Here is a single verse. It's about fairies, too, but of a different nature:

On the mountain peak, called "Going-To-The-Sun,"
I saw old Johnny Appleseed once more.
He ate an apple, threw away the core.
Then turned and smiled and slackly watched it fall
Into a crevice of the mountain wall.
In an instant there was an apple tree,
The roots split up the rocks beneath our feet,
And apples rolled down the green mountainside
And fairies popped from them, flying and free!

> From *Johnny Appleseed Still Further West*
> by Vachel Lindsay*

*This poem appears by permission of Nicholas Lindsay, the son of Vachel Lindsay.

Johnny, Johnny Appleseed,
　　They tell me you have gone,
With your pack upon your back
　　Through the frosty dawn;
Marching in your ragged shoes
　　Resolutely on.

Often facing grim defeat
　　Sharper than the sword
So that other hands might reap
　　Ultimate reward,
Johnny, Johnny Appleseed—
　　Servant of the Lord.

Johnny, Johnny Appleseed,
　　Dead and buried long,
We will keep your memory
　　Burning clear and strong,
And your life shall be to men—
　　A sermon and a song!

From *A Journey That Lasted a Lifetime*
by Edith Osborne Thompson

——— 🌳 ———

Yet when the Indians were on the war path, threatening his
own people, John Chapman never hesitated:

A midnight cry appals the gloom,
    The puncheon door is shaken;
"Awake! arouse! and flee the doom!
    Man, woman, child, awaken!

"Your sky shall glow with fiery beams,
    Before the morn breaks ruddy!
The scalpknife in the moonlight gleams,
    Athirst for vengeance bloody!". . .

The herald strode into the room;
    That moment, through the ashes,
The back-log struggled into bloom
    Of gold and crimson flashes.

The glimmer lighted up a face,
    And o'er a figure dartled
So eerie, of so solemn grace,
    The bluff backwoodsman startled . . .

"Farewell! I go!—the forest calls
    My life to ceaseless labors;
Wherever danger's shadow falls
    I fly to save my neighbors.". . .

From *Johnny Appleseed, a Ballad of the Old Northwest*
by William Henry Venable

[John was a scout in the War of 1812.] When peace came
again:

Day in, day out, and year by year,
From Licking Creek to the far frontier,
Johnny Appleseed comes and goes,
Comrade of every wind that blows;
The hills are his and the winding streams,
His bark canoe, and his cherished dreams.

Sharing the settler's meager fare,
Leaving his peace and blessing there;
Stopping to be the Indian's guest—
But onward ever, face to the West,
With his sack of seeds he goes again,
Planting his orchards for other men.

Johnny Appleseed, fare you well!
Children's children have lived to tell
How their fathers trekked to the frontier's hem
And found your orchards awaiting them;
How their mothers wept with joy to see
The blossoming boughs of an apple tree,
And hearts took root in the alien loam,
And every orchard became a home.

From *Johnny Appleseed* by Florence Boyce Davis

—— 🌳 ——

The long trail and its ending are the theme of a number of verses:

He traveled far, yet bore no sword or withe,
Evangelist to him who tilled the sod,
Forlorn and poor, yet gratefully his tithe
Though jot and tittle he returned to God.

Of pence and script so small amount his store
Time would be pillaged to indite the whole,
But on his brow the morning's light he wore;
At dusk he watched the firmament unroll
To set the planets voyaging through space;
The clouds, those mystic islands of the air,
Let fall their soothing moisture on his face,
And lodged their shining drops upon his hair. . . .

Aged and gray, beside the postern door
Where restful twilights breathe a vesper song
The lonely wayfarer went forth no more
But lay him down—the journey had been long;
Above his couch of moveless slumber glow
The stars like roses turned to silver ash,
A solitary pine tree bending low
Tempers the wind and the lightning's flash. . . .

The quaint apostle of the trackless wood
Has fared a last unbroken pathway—home.

From *Evensong* by Rosa A. Langtry

51

From the hillside's ordered orchard trees and from the
chimney stones,
Where the gnarled old stump puts forth a clump of bloom
to hide its bones,
Each tree tells Johnny Appleseed that the trails he loved to
tread
Still are wild and sweet where he set his feet, long after he
is dead.
God bless you, Johnny Appleseed, when the blossoms hum
with bees,
And bless you, saint of the burlap sack, when the red fruit
weights the trees;

For the sack of seeds, and the tinpan hat that the settlers
reckoned queer
Cast a shadow over this land of yours that lengthens year
by year,
And now that a century's come and gone, you, gentle,
selfless, meek,
Are enshrined in the hearts of those that dwell where once
you set your feet.

From *Johnny Appleseed* by Gertrude H. Martin

Afterwards:

When April flings her tender green
    Through all the old Northwest,
When apple orchards spread their bloom
    Across the country's breast,
There be some dreamers who declare
    That through spring sun and rain
The wraith of Johnny Appleseed,
Strange zealot Johnny Appleseed,
Clear-visioned Johnny Appleseed,
    Swings down the trails again.

When Jonathans and Winesaps hang
    Like rubies in the trees,
And smooth Grimes Goldens simulate
    Fruit of Hesperides,
There be some dreamers who aver
    That, topping the hill's crest,
The wraith of Johnny Appleseed,
Queer, tattered Johnny Appleseed,
Far-seeing Johnny Appleseed,
    Strides singing toward the west.

Song for the Apple Orchards
by B. Y. Williams

—— 🌳 ——

The career of John Chapman as a symbol of the fruitful life
of man is touched upon by various poets, but seldom as ef-
fectively as in the impressive Foundation Day Ceremonial of
Indiana University, near the region where he completed his
life's labors. It is set to music for Chorus and Orchestra.
The audience bows in prayer:

> Oh, Father in Heaven, Thy sunshine and rain
> Send down on these plantings of our daily joy and pain!
> Grant fruitage a thousandfold for all our fellowmen,
> And rest 'neath the stars until the morning come again!
>
> Oh, Father in Heaven, Thy holy angels send
> To guide our homeward journey till Thy smile shall crown
> the end!
> As orchards in springtime may our lives be fragrant then,
> When Heaven gleams through death, and when the
> morning comes again!
>
> Oh, Father in Heaven, hear Thou our evening prayer!
> Oh, grant us, until the harvest strip our branches bare,
> To walk in the sunlight of Eternity, and then
> To rest 'neath the stars until Thy morning come again!

The Prayer of John Chapman by William Chauncy Langdon
Music by Charles Diven Campbell

—— 🌳 ——

Writers and poets have seized upon the intriguing subject of "Johnny Appleseed" with enthusiasm and are represented by a total of nearly six-hundred items, as found in a recently issued bibliography,[1] while for those who work in other mediums, the possibilities lie mostly in the future. There have been a few productions, however, in the fields of music, sculpture, and painting.

The musical works are in the nature of settings to poems of various types and are listed in connection with those in this anthology; to which must be added the cantata for treble voices by Harvey B. Gaul. One production has achieved official top rank—the oratorio setting by Eunice Kettering of Vachel Lindsay's "In Praise of Johnny Appleseed" received a First Award in the 1943 contest of the National Federation of Music Clubs and was broadcast over a nationwide hook-up.

The Johnny Appleseed Overture, winner of a national competition sponsored by the Woman's Auxiliary of the Toledo Orchestra Association to commemorate Ohio's sesquicentennial, was given its first performance March 1, 1953, by the Toledo Orchestra with Wolfgang Stressmann conducting.

Competition for the $500 prize was open to native Ohioans, present legal residents, and persons who had ten years' residence in the state. The winning composer was Albert Sendry, of Los Angeles, who lived in Cleveland from 1912 to 1923. Jurors were Karl Ahrendt, director of the School of Music at Ohio University, Athens, Ohio; David Robertson, director of the Oberlin Conservatory of Music, Oberlin, Ohio; and Beryl Rubenstein, director of the Cleveland Institute of Music.

A sculptured group by Edward Amateis for the American Folklore exhibit of the New York World's Fair, held in 1939, featured the pioneer nurseryman, as does a figure executed by Anna Coleman Ladd.

In the field of painting, two canvases, which are in the modern manner, include a mural by Anton Refregier, in the Plainfield, New Jersey, post office, and an oil by Doris Lee.

The illustrations by various artists that accompany many of the magazine articles about Johnny Appleseed must not be overlooked, for there is considerable variety in conception and technique. The oldest probably is the quaint woodcut, said to have been made from a sketch by a student at Oberlin College from a description, and first printed in the *History of Richland Co., Ohio* in 1880.[2] The important early account in *Harper's Monthly Magazine,* November 1871, is illustrated apparently by two artists, the drawings being of considerable charm, as shown in the woodcuts. Line drawings accompany a number of the later magazine articles and some of the poems. Two are illustrated in color.

These portrayals, like those of the poets, show the many-sided nature of the earnest evangelist: the hard-working nurseryman; the friend of Indians, children, and creatures of the wild; the backwoodsman; and hero of various exploits.

Carvings of Ohio historical scenes form the backs of a series of settees exhibited at the Century of Progress Exposition, Chicago, 1933–1934, one showing Johnny Appleseed and his beloved trees, are now in the Ashland, Ohio, Public Library.[3]

In the not-too-distant future, not only will the artist find Johnny Appleseed a fascinating subject, but the motion picture will bring our pioneer friend to life on the screen before our delighted eyes.

——— 🌳 ———

Since the first edition of this book in 1945, the centennial of Johnny Appleseed's death, we have learned of many more things that are serving to keep his memory much alive. Even the prediction of an important screen appearance has materialized. One of the lengthy episodes in Walt Disney's *Melody Time*, in 1948, featured Johnny, as portrayed by singer Dennis Day.[4] It was a charming and lively musical version of his adventures with the little forest people and the pioneers, along his apple-planting trails in the Ohio Country.

But Johnny today travels farther than that, and sometimes in high company, too. For some years, the U.S. Liberty Ship *Johnny Appleseed* has been sailing the seven seas, calling at the most remote ports of the world, under the command of Captain A. C. Allen.

In 1951, a famous $1,250 Steuben glass Bowl of American Legends, designed by Sidney Waugh, and portraying our friend among other characters, was sent by the President of the United States as a wedding gift to the Shah of Persia. And listed in the *Journal of American Folklore* in 1949, as one of the "culture heroes," along with such greats as Aeneas, Prometheus, Moses, Krishna, and Franklin, we find our humble Johnny Appleseed.

Art and science have united in producing the Johnny Appleseed Medal, designed by the distinguished Edmond

Amateis for the Men's Garden Club of America, to replace its certificate annually awarded to the man who has given the most altruistic service in horticulture. The first recipient of the medal was Dr. Liberty Hyde Bailey, on his ninetieth birthday.

Johnny's "likeness" appears in a stained glass window of a large Episcopal Church in Pittsburgh, and in the Union Church, Kenilworth, Illinois. In Cincinnati, he has been seen as a marionette, and, in the shops of many large cities, on fabrics, wallpaper, towels, tablemats, plates and notepaper. His name is borne by a D.A.R. chapter in West Virginia; a general store in N. Beverly, Massachusetts; bookstores in Manchester, Vermont, and Mansfield, Ohio, as well as the high school and coffee shop in the latter place.

Birthday parties, dramatics, editorials, broadcasts, pageants, lectures, sermons, booklets, newspaper and magazine articles, books for children, poems, and references in histories, continue unabated, with probable acceleration in 1953, the sesquicentennial year of the State of Ohio, the scene of most of Johnny's self-sacrificing labors. The governors of that great commonwealth twice have proclaimed a "Johnny Appleseed Day," commemorating his birthday in 1941 and 1946.

The State of Indiana, the locale of Johnny's last years and death, honored his memory on May 20, 1949, by the dedication of a 250-acre park near Fort Wayne, which includes the two disputed burial places, as well as an adjoining highway bridge over the St. Joseph river. Dr. Robert Price, author of the first chapter in this book, and Governor Shricker of Indiana were the principal speakers.

How astonished Johnny would have been at the impressive ceremonies, the presence of the governor and his staff, the city officials, the flags flying and the bands playing![5]

Editor's Update

1. The author is referring to Robert Price's *John Chapman: A Bibliography of Johnny Appleseed in History, Literature and Folklore* (Patterson, N.J.: The Swedenborg Press, 1944).

2. The earliest known printing of this image served as the frontispiece in H. S. Knapp's *A History of the Pioneer and Modern Times of Ashland County, Ohio* (Philadelphia: J. B. Lippincott & Co., 1863). It depicted a gaunt and barefooted John Chapman with pasteboard cap of his own design, unusual suspender, and Bible or Swedenborg tract tucked in the blouse of his shirt. Rosella Rice described him the same way, but it is unknown which was developed first, her description or the image. The head gear was eventually changed to a broad brimmed floppy hat as depicted in A. A. Graham's *History of Richland County, Ohio* (Mansfield, Ohio: 1880).

3. This particular Johnny Appleseed settee is currently exhibited in the Ashland County Historical Society Museum, Ashland, Ohio.

4. *Melody Time* (including its Johnny Appleseed episode) was released by Walt Disney Home Video on VHS video tape in 1998.

5. Additions continue to mount:
   In Ohio, alone: Mansfield's Johnny Appleseed Junior High School was erected in 1939; an image of Johnny Appleseed is on both a chariot and an upper mural of a carousel in Carousel Park; a modern raised sculpture adorns the front of FirstMerit Bank; the

Johnny Appleseed District of the Heart of Ohio Boy Scouts of America offers its Johnny Appleseed Trail, for which completion of its route earns credit toward the Order of the Arrow; and the city has a Johnny Appleseed Shopping Center. Proclamations by Ohio Governor Bob Taft and mayors and county commissioners of Mansfield (Richland County) and Mount Vernon (Knox County) designated September 26, 1999, Johnny Appleseed Day and the last week in September 1999 Johnny Appleseed Week. Events surrounded two historic markers dedications and a running relay between the two communities to commemorate Johnny's famous barefooted midnight run for reinforcements during the War of 1812. Mount Vernon dedicated an earlier marker in memory of its first permanent settler and Chapman's early associated nursery site.

The Johnny Appleseed Heritage Center and Outdoor Historical Drama is developing a 1,600-seat amphitheater on a 45-acre wooded site near Mansfield, Ohio, to enhance its theatrical play on Chapman's life. Plans call for a museum, a classroom, The J. M. Smucker Auditorium and Library, nature trails, an antique orchard, the Johnny Appleseed Country Eco-Heritage Corridor, and scenic by-ways. In conjunction with the Muskingum Watershed Conservancy District, the center dedicated 118 acres as Johnny Appleseed Forest, on May 19, 2000.

The Johnny Appleseed Society and Museum has been developed at Urbana University in Urbana, Ohio.

There are also the Johnny Appleseed Trail of North Central Massachusetts, which links commercial and recreational resources along a heritage corridor; and the Johnny Appleseed Festival, in Johnny Appleseed Memorial Park, Fort Wayne, Indiana, the largest of countless Appleseed festivals that are held throughout the country.

Even New Zealand has its own fruit-packing plant named in Johnny Appleseed's honor. A retired Ohio school teacher who was born and educated in Austria remembers learning about Johnny

Appleseed in elementary school. They have heard of him in Australia, too.

And finally, to prove practically everyone wants to claim Johnny for their very own, Lakewood High School's main entrance, Lakewood, Ohio, has a raised sculpture of early local pioneer and horticulturist Jared Kirtland in a planting posture. For years, it has affectionately, but mistakenly, been referred to as the Johnny Appleseed mural!

The Religion of Johnny Appleseed

by John W. Stockwell

Johnny Appleseed was the Francis of Assisi of Protestantism. But he was also a John the Baptist, for he was "a voice crying in the wilderness" heralding the beginning of a new Christianity—a religion for mankind in maturity, a "New Jerusalem, coming down from God out of heaven" to earth.

Thus, he had his humble part in the coming fulfillment of prophecy in that biblical book of ecstatic beauty and beatific splendor—Revelation.

In John Chapman, service and sacrifice were sanctified. He was the mystic of the mountain top, bringing to mind the words from Isaiah 52:7: "How beautiful upon the mountains are the feet of him that bringeth good tidings, that publisheth peace; that bringeth good tidings of good, that publisheth salvation; that saith unto Zion, Thy God Reigneth."

Johnny's feet, often unshod, pressed intimately upon the good earth. He was a prophet to those of humble circumstance. He brought to them an elixir of life for the soul—to the lonely and the lowly—among America's pioneer pathways.

Yes—chiefly—Johnny Appleseed was a herald of the kingdom of heaven. Even while he trod on earthly soil, his mind was already exploring the New Jerusalem's streets of gold!

His thoughts inhabited the Christian faith, which can be so substantial and so interiorly coherent that it is indeed "four-square"—for both mind and soul. That is what the New Jerusalem of faith meant to him—"coming down from God out of heaven, prepared as a bride adorned for her husband"—the Christian religion grown up to rationality and a rational philosophy redeemed by religion.

For the religion of the race has indeed had a growth like that of a human being.

I

One cannot understand John Chapman ("Johnny Appleseed") unless one understands his religion. Here is a human being so aglow with reality that he is shining more and more brightly through the veil of vagary and misconception.

His life was a perfect exemplification of the four rules of life which Emanuel Swedenborg laid down for himself. Daily, Johnny obeyed the first rule: "Often to read and meditate on the Word of God." Thus, he prepared himself to sow the seeds of truth wherever he went.

He had no frustrations, no fears, no conflicts within his soul, for he lived according to Swedenborg's second rule of life: "To submit everything to the will of Divine Providence." He was content to be the instrument of that power, confident in the strength of the Lord.

Johnny was scrupulously honest, and never was he guilty of improper conduct. He kept the third rule of life: "To observe in everything a propriety of behavior and to keep the conscience clear." By example and precept, he pointed the way to the good life—a life of use.

Swedenborg's fourth rule of life was: "To obey what is commanded, to discharge with fidelity the functions of my employment and the duties of my office, and to render myself in all things useful to society." Faithfully, Johnny spread the doctrines of Swedenborg, and usefully he planted his apple seeds and cared for his nurseries. Had not the Lord said that a seed would serve him?

Johnny Appleseed served his fellow humans in sickness, in sorrow, in times of danger. All were his brothers and sisters, be their skins red, black, or white. Truly, he discharged with fidelity the duties of his employment and rendered himself in all things useful to society. He said to the weak, "Fear not." He made glad the solitary places. He made the wilderness rejoice and bear fruit.

II

The theology "Johnny Appleseed" adopted is known as "Swedenborgian." It was formulated by Emanuel Swedenborg (1688–1772) who is recognized today by leading scientists and philosophers and by some of the foremost theologians as having had one of the most thoroughly all-around developed minds of all history. His father was court chaplain and a bishop of the Swedish State Church; his diocese included the early Swedish settlement in America, along the Delaware River.

Swedenborg, in his later years, became profoundly interested in straightening out in his own mind the Christian doctrines. He studied the Bible in the original Hebrew and Greek. He concluded that the parable method of teaching in the New Testament was also that of the Old Testament; that there is an inner, inspired meaning not only in Matthew, Mark, Luke, John, and Revelation of the New Testament but also in the twenty-nine books of the Old Testament, which on their face declared themselves to be of divine authority. The relationship between the literal and the spiritual meaning was named correspondences—the one corresponding to the other, although on different levels of meaning and value.

Johnny Appleseed also wholeheartedly accepted and passed along to many Swedenborg's other central teachings that the Lord Jesus Christ is the one God of heaven and earth; that there is an unbroken continuity of life, with the world of the spirit near and real; that reformation requires a life of useful service and self-denial.

Swedenborg did not found a church. However, his early followers in England, finding his books so inspiring and clarifying, formed groups for their study, and that was the beginning of the organized body now known as the Church of the New Jerusalem.

III

We have examined somewhat the doctrinal ideas with which Chapman fed his mind and inspired his soul to heroic service for the Lord and his fellow human beings. Now come closer to John Chapman as child and youth, and see the seeding and cultivating of his religious life.

His mother, Elizabeth Simonds of Leominster, Massachusetts, died July 18, 1776. A little over a month before her death, the mother had written a letter to her "loving husband," then in New York in "Captain Pollard's Company of Carpenters" Continental Army—and soul-revealing it was!

> Our children are both well through the Divine Goodness . . . and I rejoice to hear that you are well and I pray you may thus continue and in God's due time be returned in safety. . . . I am under the care of a kind Providence who is able to do more for me than I can ask or think, and I desire humbly to submit to His Holy Will with patience and resignation. . . . My cough is somewhat abated, but think I grow weaker. I desire your prayers for me, that I may be prepared for the will of God, that I may so improve my remainder of life that I may answer the great end for which I was made, that I might glorify God here and finally come to the enjoyment of him in a world of glory. . . . Remember, I beseech you, that you are a mortal and that you must submit to death sooner or later and consider that we are always in danger of our spiritual enemy. Be, therefore, on your guard continually, and live in a daily preparation for death—and so I must bid you farewell and if it should be so ordered that I should not see you again, I hope we shall both be as happy as to spend an eternity of happiness together in the coming world which is my desire and prayer.

Robert C. Harris, [former] secretary of the Johnny Appleseed Memorial Commission of Fort Wayne, Indiana, records
that this letter is a true copy of the original in the possession
of Kittie Dix Humphrey of Detroit, Michigan.[1]

John Chapman, as a baby, with a sister not quite four
years older and later with ten stepbrothers and sisters, developed—there can be no question about it—an extremely sen-
sitive nature. He must also have acquired during those early
years an affection full, empowering, and surcharged with a
growing understanding of his mother's selfless love. Evidently, too, he developed a mind attuned to testimony (received later in the New Church teaching) as to the reality
and nearness of that heavenly home to which his mother
had gone.

Chapman became a witness to the truth in John
Greenleaf Whittier's lines of transcendent wisdom:

> There sometimes comes to soul and sense
> > A feeling which is evidence
> That very near about us lies
> > The world of spirit mysteries.

Upon such a soul with such a childhood overcharged
with the sacred drama of motherhood known—oh, so
briefly—and then lost awhile but never gone—upon such a
soul came the doctrines of the New Church, centered
around enduring love and so softly and sweetly assuring as
to the heavenly home; so, Johnny Appleseed's philosophy is
born. It is partly full-grown and partly clinging about the
celestial glories that only "childhood" can make true-to-life,
those of the New Testament's literal messages:

"Blessed are the meek: for they shall inherit the earth.

"Blessed are the pure in heart: for they shall see God."

(John Chapman's favorite Bible verses)

So John Chapman, "Johnny Appleseed," by the urge of that great but so often unrecognized and more often misunderstood spiritual psychology becomes the evangelist, proclaiming news fresh from heaven to bring peace to men of good will on earth:

Glory to God in the highest, and on earth peace, good will toward men. (Luke 2:14)

The biographer gauges John Chapman as America's pioneer planter of apple trees and dispenser of doctrine expounded by Swedenborg.

But the future will find in him an influence that helped America see the real glory of Christianity revealed in the inner meaning of Sacred Scripture.

Editor's Update

1. The ownership and location of this rare document are unknown today.

The Story of Johnny Appleseed

by Ophia D. Smith

*T*he people of old Spain had a maxim that whoever eats a fruit must plant the seed; otherwise, he is ungrateful to the past and unjust to the coming generation. Whenever a Spaniard ate a fruit, he dug a hole in the ground with his toe, placed the seed therein, and scraped a bit of earth over it with his foot. As a consequence, there was an abundance of fruit in Spain to be had for the taking, along highways and in remote places. The Spaniard who should be credited with this practical idea has been forgotten, but the name of the man who did more than any other to plant orchards in the old northwest is widely known. His parents gave him the name of John Chapman; those who loved him for his kindly deeds called him "Johnny Appleseed."

For fifty years, this rugged old pioneer toiled along the water-courses and wilderness trails to provide apple trees for the immigrants who came west, and to spread the

doctrines of Emanuel Swedenborg. Even his name possesses
a certain significance, for "John" literally means "Jehovah
hath been gracious," and "Chapman" means an itinerant
merchant who, in colonial days, carried chapbooks of a religious nature among his wares. Johnny Appleseed was a
chapman who carried Swedenborgian tracts and books to
give away to anyone who would read them.

As those who knew him passed from earthly to spiritual life, Johnny became a legendary figure; and although
some of his friends and acquaintances wrote down their recollections of him and the work he did, these stories, "begot
in the ventricle of memory" and written "upon the mellow-
ing of occasion," now frequently confound the researcher.
To separate truth from fancy often is well-nigh impossible.

Only recently has the ancestry of John Chapman been
established. It is now known that John was a direct descendant of Edward Chapman, who came from Yorkshire, England, to Boston in the 1640s and became a prosperous
farmer and miller in Ipswich. John was of the sixth generation from Edward. He was the second child of Elizabeth Simonds and Nathaniel Chapman who were married at
Leominster, Massachusetts, on February 8, 1770. John was
born at Leominster on September 26, 1774, and was bap-
tized with his sister Elizabeth in the Congregational Church
on June 25, 1775, the day his father and mother were received into that church. John's father, Nathaniel, was a car-
penter, a farmer, and a Revolutionary War soldier. So far as
any records show, he was a man of little means, though
there is a tradition that he lost two good farms in the service
of his country.

A letter from Elizabeth to Nathaniel, dated June 3,
1776, suggests that she was suffering from an advanced case

of tuberculosis [see previous article by John W. Stockwell]. At that time, Nathaniel was with a company of carpenters attached to General Washington's headquarters at New York. In this letter, Elizabeth stated that she had money for her needs, although she had not bought a cow, for cows were scarce and dear. This was a time of hardship and wartime inflation when many a colonial mother had a hard time caring for her children.

On June 26, 1776, Elizabeth gave birth to her third child, a son. On July 18, she died, and within two weeks, according to family tradition, the baby, too, was dead. Little John, not yet two years old, and his sister Elizabeth were cared for, presumably, by kind relatives. After Elizabeth's death, Nathaniel continued to serve in the Continental Army.

In the summer of 1780, Nathaniel Chapman, captain of wheelwrights under Major Eayres, was honorably discharged from the army.[1] In the summer, he was married to Lucy Cooley of Longmeadow, Massachusetts. To them were born ten children.*

Whether Elizabeth's children went to live with Nathaniel and Lucy or not, John sustained intimate relations with the family. According to family tradition, John, at the age of eighteen, persuaded his half-brother Nathaniel, a lad of eleven, to go west with him. This was in 1792.†

Since the deeply worn "Connecticut Path" from Boston to Albany crossed the Connecticut River at

---

*Florence E. Wheeler, "John Chapman's Line of Descent from Edward Chapman of Ipswich," *Ohio State Archaeological and Historical Quarterly* XLVIII, 21, 39–41; Robert Price, "The New England Origins of Johnny Appleseed," *New England Quarterly* XII, 454–469.

†Anna Long Onstott, *New Church Messenger,* Sept. 30, 1942.

Springfield, one may presume that the boys saw emigrants passing to the West every day and that they constantly heard glowing stories of that wonderful land. For almost half a century, New Englanders had turned longing eyes toward the Susquehanna. They had first heard of it from missionaries returned in their efforts to convert the Indians to the Christian faith. These stories spread throughout Connecticut and Massachusetts by word of mouth and through the press. Little companies of emigrants were organized, and they set out for the fabulous country two hundred miles away, crossing the Hudson River at about where the present town of Catskill stands. This was just half way to the Susquehanna. Under the most favorable conditions, it took two or three weeks of the hardest kind of travel and labor to reach the headwaters of the Susquehanna.*

John Chapman is said to have been in the Wilkes-Barre region some time in the 1790s,[2] practicing his profession as a nurseryman;† just when he embraced the Swedenborgian faith and began his missionary activities we cannot be sure, although it is probable that it was before he ever reached western Pennsylvania.[3] Two or three writers who knew Johnny Appleseed say that he sometimes spoke of his activities as "a Bible Missionary" on the Potomac when he was a young man. One writer claims that Johnny was seen for two or three successive years along the banks of the Potomac in eastern Virginia, picking the seeds from the pumice of the cider mills, in the late 1790s.‡

---

*Anna Long Onstott, *New Church Messenger,* Sept. 30, 1942.
†Price, "A Boyhood for Johnny Appleseed," *New England Quarterly* XVII, 393; W. M. Glines, *Johnny Appleseed by One Who Knew Him* (Columbus, Ohio: 1922).
‡Geo. Wm. Hill, *History of Ashland County* (Ashland, Ohio: 1880), 184.

From the Potomac, he could have worked his way westward to Fort Cumberland. From Fort Cumberland, he could have followed Nemacolin's Path, better known as Braddock's Road, to the Monongahela, and followed the Monongahela to Pittsburgh, a route that many New Englanders took because there were fewer Indians to be encountered along the southern route.

When Johnny was only ten years old (1784), George Washington traveled this road to survey the possibilities of the West. On that trip, he saw the "fingertips of the Potomac" reaching toward the Youghiogheny and the Monongahela, and caught the vision of canals and portage roads to join the Hudson, the Susquehanna, the Potomac, and the James. John Chapman, too, caught a vision of the future development of the West as he traversed the wilderness. It is said that he procured his seeds from the settlers along the Monongahela to plant his nurseries at Braddock's Field, at Wheeling, on the Grave Creek Flats, at Holliday's Cove, and that he returned there for seeds.[*]

From Pittsburgh, according to one story, the Chapman boys went up the Allegheny River to its confluence with Olean Creek at Olean, New York. They expected to find an uncle there, but he had moved on. The boys appropriated the cabin and stayed through the winter, suffering much hardship. The next year, they again took up their nomadic life in western Pennsylvania until their father, with his large family, went west in 1805.[†] Presumably, the Chapmans

---

[*]General Roeliff Brinkerhoff, Scrapbook, Clipping No. 21, a letter from S. C. Coffinberry to editor of the Mansfield, Ohio, *Shield and Banner*, dated Constantine, Michigan, Nov. 23, 1871. The Brinkerhoff Scrapbook is in the Library, Ohio State Arch. and Hist. Museum, Columbus, Ohio.
[†]Price, "A Boyhood for Johnny Appleseed," 392.

lived at Marietta while the boys cleared a farm on Duck Creek. Nathaniel, senior, had plenty of manpower in his family to clear and plant and build. The fertile soil of the Muskingum Valley offered a marked contrast to the stony fields of Massachusetts.

Johnny, however, went up and down the Muskingum and its tributaries planting his apple seeds from the Monongahela. By instinct, he practiced the Van Mons theory of improving fruit by seeding rather than by grafting or budding.* He was not unique in that he planted seedling nurseries. Many early nurserymen planted seeds, but they did not itinerate as he did. In 1790, Ebenezer Zane had an extensive seedling nursery in Zanesville. There were some small orchards, of course, planted by the Indians from the seeds of the fine orchards of the French traders and missionaries.

Johnny Appleseed went ahead of the great immigrant flood ever sweeping westward. He planted with an eye to future markets, and seldom did he make a poor choice. It is uncanny how many towns have risen on or near his nursery sites. Had he used that native shrewdness to make money for himself, he might have been considered a man of substance, rather than an eccentric old man who planted apple seeds; but then he would never have become the subject of song and story and the object of veneration that he is today.

John Chapman appeared on Licking Creek, in what is now Licking County, Ohio, in 1800, when he was twenty-six years old. He had probably come up the Muskingum River to plant near the Refugee Tract, which would soon fill up with settlers, when Congress actually got around to

---

Ohio Cultivator, Sept. 1, 1846.

granting the lands. In April 1798, the Continental Congress had ratified resolutions to donate public lands for the benefit of those who had left Canada and Nova Scotia to fight against the British in the Revolutionary War. The lands were actually set apart in 1801 and patents issued in 1802. Grants of land ranging from 160 acres to 2,240 acres were awarded according to the exertions of the patentee in the war. Johnny, with true Yankee enterprise, went ahead and planted his nurseries before the refugees arrived. Licking County, then a part of Fairfield, contained only three white families. When William Stanberry came, in 1809, to settle near the confluence of the Muskingum River and Licking Creek, Johnny Appleseed's trees were ready for the market.

At Stanberry's house, Johnny often spent the night, usually sleeping out in a grove near the house. Stanberry said that Johnny ate only vegetables. Some of Johnny's friends have said that he was very fond of milk and honey, because he considered them heavenly foods.

Chapman was always eager to make converts to the New Church. It seemed to be his "main business" to "leave the books wherever he could get anybody to read them." Johnny was always delighted to find a family that was eager for something to read. One of the books that Johnny carried with him was Swedenborg's *Heaven and Hell*. As the Stanberrys and Johnny read together Swedenborg's description of hell, they agreed that it described accurately the town of Newark. At that time, Newark was largely given over to horse-racing and hard liquor.

Johnny was thoroughly familiar with his Bible and the writings of Swedenborg. There was nothing he liked better than a theological argument. He could present his thesis with cogency and penetration. To him, the Swedenborgian idea of the future life was amazingly simple. He said once to William Stanberry's brother, "It is no more mysterious to me or even to you that you should live in different zones after death than that you live in them now." When asked by John Vandorn of Richland County what he would do for a living in the next world, he replied, "Well, I will follow the same occupation as I do here, but with more pleasure and happiness."*

Johnny Appleseed must have been one of the earliest Swedenborgians in America. The first General Convention of the New Jerusalem in the United States of America met in Philadelphia in May 1817. Four months prior to the Convention, a report of Johnny's labors was published in Manchester, England. At the Fifth General Convention, also held in Philadelphia, Johnny Appleseed's missionary work was again reported at some length. In a letter dated Philadelphia, May 15, 1821, Daniel Thunn wrote to Margaret Bailey at Cincinnati:

> . . . To add something more to the New Church news, there is Mr. John Chapman near Wooster, Ohio, who wrote lately to Mr. Schlatter that he found an increase of Receivers all around his neighborhood and that they are spreading as far as Detroit, he proposed to make a Deed over to the New Church for a Quarter Section of Land and take payment in Books of the New Church. We

---

*N. N. Hill, *History of Licking County* (Newark, Ohio, 1881), 239–240; Joshua Antrim, *History of Champaign and Logan Counties from Their First Settlement* (Bellefontaine, 1872), 149–153; F. B. Pearson and J. D. Harlor, *Ohio History Sketches* (Columbus, 1903), 52; Henry Howe, *Historical Collections of Ohio* (2 vols., Cincinnati, 1904), II, 69; Letter, written by John H. James, Jan. 23, 1857, from Urbana, Ohio, to the Cincinnati Horticultural Society; Brinkerhoff Scrapbook, Clipping No. 20.

contemplate how best to fulfill his wishes. This is the Appleseed man you certainly must have heard of, who goes around in the Country to plant Apple Trees.

This letter seems to bear out the tradition that Johnny Appleseed had nurseries planted around Richmond, Indiana, when the first settlers arrived. Already, in 1804, a few families were pushing into "the gore" along the Whitewater River in Indiana Territory. The Greenville Treaty Line (1795) established a boundary that ran from Lake Erie by way of the Cuyahoga and Tuscarawas Rivers westward to Fort Recovery (Greenville, Ohio) and southwestward to the Ohio, opposite the mouth of the Kentucky River, thus forming a gore-shaped tract on the Indian side of the Ohio state line. At least one Methodist preacher settled on Elkhorn Creek near the present town of Richmond in 1805. By 1808, a circuit-rider was covering Indiana Territory as far north as Richmond and westward across Indiana and Illinois Territories, and across the Mississippi River into Missouri.* If the Methodists found enough settlers to warrant so much activity, there was undoubtedly a market for apple trees. In his role as a precursor of the frontier, Johnny could have come to Cincinnati down the Ohio a few miles, and up the Whitewater into the vicinity of Richmond. It is claimed that the earliest settlers around Richmond knew Johnny Appleseed and that he stopped in their cabins.

---

*Helen V. Austin, "Johnny Appleseed, the Pioneer Pomologist of the West," *Indiana Horticultural Society Transactions* XXII, 35–40, reprinted in *Missouri State Horticultural Society Annual Report* XXXIII, 13–18; Wm. C. Smith, *Indiana Miscellany* (Cincinnati, 1867), 49–51; *History of Wayne County, Indiana* (2 vols., Chicago, 1884), I, 355; "Johnny Appleseed, a Pioneer Benefactor" in 1840–1940 series in Richmond (Ind.) Palladium, 1940.

According to W. M. Glines, who knew the Chapman family, Johnny Appleseed planted a nursery on the school lands at Delaware, Ohio; made a small improvement there; and went on to Sandusky. He might have followed the Warrior's Path (Cumberland Gap–Sandusky) which was the shortest way between Delaware and Sandusky and a route likely to be traveled by immigrants. From Sandusky, he could have followed the Sandusky–Pittsburgh Trail to the Forks of the Mohican. In this region, Johnny made his headquarters for some time. That he had several nurseries on the Mohican is evident from an order written by him: "Due John Oliver one hundred and fifty trees when he goes for them to some of my nurseries on Mohecin waters."[*]

Johnny Appleseed was seen in 1806, floating down the Ohio River with two canoes lashed together and filled with apple seeds. Upon landing at Steubenville, he announced that he had come to plant his seeds. He planted his first nursery in Jefferson County not far from Steubenville at what is now the town of Brilliant. This was a logical place for a nursery, for under the Harrison Land Law of 1800, Steubenville was one of the four Ohio land offices, where a settler could buy land at two dollars an acre, making a down payment of only fifty cents an acre.[†]

John Chapman came into the Firelands with the first settlers, or what was already there, in 1811. The Firelands, a tract of land that constitutes Huron County, was granted by

---

[*]E. O. Randall, ed., "'Johnny Appleseed' Addendum," *Ohio State Arch. and Hist. Pub.* (Columbus, 1901), IX, 315.
[†]W. H. Hunter, "The Pathfinders of Jefferson County," *Ohio State Arch. and Hist. Pub.*, VI, 291; Dana Elbert Clark, *The West in American History* (New York, 1937), 248.

Connecticut (1792) to certain citizens of that state whose homes had been burned or otherwise laid waste in the Revolutionary War. Caleb Palmer, a surveyor, came into the Firelands in 1810 and returned with a man named Woodcock in 1811, just two years after Huron County was formed. Johnny Appleseed made his home at Palmer's for some time and was intimately associated with Palmer and Woodcock.*

Johnny Appleseed had the satisfaction of seeing the last tree from his Firelands nurseries set out, and some of his neighbors had to go to one of his nurseries in Delaware County to secure apple trees for planting.† Johnny helped these hardy pioneers with their work, as he went among them telling about his apple trees and of "the good news right fresh from Heaven." Some writers say that he was a cranberry peddler. Thousands of bushels of cranberries were harvested from the marshes of the Firelands by squatters and sold to remote settlers. Cranberries, huckleberries, "shack pork," wild meat, coonskins, and produce from small potato patches constituted most of the frontier currency.‡ Wherever Johnny Appleseed went, he paid his own way.

He had unusual ideas about charging for his trees and collecting for them. He would take a reasonable price in money, some cast-off clothing, a bit of food, or nothing at all, according to the circumstances of his customer. To him, it was more important for a settler to plant a tree than to pay for it. He never liked to have a note dated for a specific day; for, said he, it might not be convenient to collect

---

*A. G. Stewart, "Memoirs of Townships. New Haven," *Firelands Pioneer* I, 9; Mrs. H. J. Heller, "New Haven," *Firelands Pioneer* XV, 1081.
†"Greenfield in 1819," *Firelands Pioneer* XI, 89.
‡Heller, "New Haven," 1074.

that day, or it might not be convenient for the customer to pay on that date. He never asked a man to pay a debt, for he reasoned that, if God wanted him to have the money, God would move the customer to pay. Besides, the customer knew that he owed the money, without being reminded of it.

Chapman was methodical in the selection of his nursery sites and the planting of his seeds. He always selected a good loamy piece of ground in an open place, fenced it in with fallen trees and logs, bushes, and vines; sowed his seeds; and returned at regular intervals to repair the fence, to tend the ground, and to sell his trees. If he had to remain long with a nursery, he put up a little Indian hut of poles and covered it with a bark roof, leaving a hole in the center for the smoke to escape. His housekeeping equipment consisted of a camp kettle, a plate, and a spoon. He sometimes made a bed of leaves inside the hut, but often he slept on the bare ground with his feet to a small fire. Sometimes he slept on a bed of leaves beside a log; again, he might make himself a temporary shelter by leaning great slabs of elm bark against a fallen tree; inside, on his bed of leaves, he slept serenely, confident that nothing could harm him. Men came from long distances to buy trees from him and then stayed the night. With his meager equipment, Johnny boiled mush and dispensed hospitality as graciously as any housewife.*

When Johnny put out a large nursery, he sometimes erected a small log cabin for his use, inviting a husky neighbor or two to assist him. Two of the Vandorn boys of the Lexington (Richland County) neighborhood went into the

---

*Hill, *History of Ashland County,* 183–187.

forest to help him raise a cabin some time after the close of the War of 1812. They arrived one evening about dusk. Johnny was standing close to a fire kindled by the side of a large log. He was very glad to see them. There he was, four miles from a living soul, except Indians, among catamounts, wolves, bears, snakes, and porcupines, yet happy and content. Five or six rods from the fire were logs already cut for a cabin and some clapboards for the roof. After sitting down and talking for a while, Johnny poked in the ashes with a stick and pulled out some roasted potatoes. From under the log he pulled a bag of salt. This simple fare he offered his guests, saying, "This is the way I live in the wilderness." He went on to say, "I could not enjoy myself better anywhere. I can lie on my back, look up at the stars, and it seems almost as though I can see the angels praising God, for he has made all things for good." One of the boys opened their sack of provisions and laid out on some clapboards bread and butter and dried venison, inviting Johnny to share it. Johnny ate some of their bread and butter, and they ate some of Johnny's baked potatoes and salt.

After the meal had been eaten, Johnny entertained the boys with stories about the Seymours and the Dutchman Ruffner. He said that the whites were to blame for all the mischief the Indians had done. He had always found the Indians friendly and kind. He told the boys about two Indians who came to his camp to tell him of a forest fire and helped him to keep it away from his camp and his nursery.

Before going to bed, the boys moved a log and discovered a rattlesnake, shaking its rattles and ready to strike. The boys wanted to kill it, but Johnny would not allow it, saying that the Indians did not kill snakes. He went on talking until the boys were sleepy. Then they lay down upon some clapboards, with their heads under Johnny's bark shed and their feet to the fire. The howling of the wolves startled the boys, and up they jumped with their guns, but Johnny said, "Tut, tut, lie down and go to sleep. I like to hear them howl." Just as the boys were again dozing off, an owl hooted. In an instant, one of the boys sprang up, gun in hand, yelling, "Indians! Indians!" Johnny only said, "Do let me sleep. I like to hear the owls hoot." He drew up his feet, turned over on his log, and in a moment was peacefully snoring.*

In the Mohican country, Johnny visited every cabin religiously, feeling that he had been commissioned to preach, to heal diseases, to warn of danger—in short, he helped God take care of the settlers. He planted his nurseries around Mansfield, Loudonville, Perrysville, and the Indian village of Green Town, living in a little cabin near Perrysville. When asked why he feared neither man nor beast, he replied that he lived in harmony with all people, and that he could not be harmed as long as he lived by the law of love. He is said to have sown the seeds of medicinal herbs wherever he went—dog fennel, pennyroyal, catnip, hoarhound, mullein, rattlesnake root, and others. For a long time, fennel was called "Johnny weed." The idea that he sowed these seeds may have come from the fact that he used them in concocting simple remedies for common ailments. He sometimes appeared at the door of a new settler's cabin with a gift of herbs in his hand.

When Johnny came to the Mohican country, Indians greatly outnumbered the white settlers. Mansfield contained only two or three cabins, and its two blockhouses were not

---

*Brinkerhoff Scrapbook, Clipping No. 20.

built until the late summer of 1812. There was a blockhouse at Beam's Mill on Rocky Fork, a picketed house belonging to Thomas Coulter on Black Fork, and a blockhouse where Ganges now stands. All supplies had to be brought in by packhorse from Mount Vernon in Knox County. It is said that when Benjamin Butler came to lay out the town of Mount Vernon in 1805, he found Johnny Appleseed already there.

Among the Indian tribes in this region were Delawares and Wyandots. There was a settlement of Delawares at Jerome's Town and one at Green Town, a village of sixty cabins and a large bark council house. There was also an Indian village nearby called Hell Town. Other Indian towns were Mohegan John's Town, Beaverhat's Town, White Woman's Town (on the Walhonding), Killbuck's Town, and Cos-hoc-ton, the Delaware capital. A number of Indian trails passed through this region, the main one being the south branch of the old Fort Duquesne-Sandusky–Detroit Trail.[*] These Indians were friendly with the whites from the time of the signing of the Treaty of Greenville in 1795 to the outbreak of the War of 1812. The Indians who stirred up the trouble in the beginning of that war were Tecumseh and his brother, the Prophet.[†]

Johnny made friends with the Indians and spoke their language. They looked upon him with a sort of superstitious awe and considered him a great medicine man. His unusual zeal for serving others led the Indians to believe him touched by the Great Spirit. For that reason, they allowed him to listen to their council meetings, and he was therefore

---

[*]I. M. Heyde, *A Brief Centennial History of Loudonville*, 6, 7.
[†]James F. M'Gaw, *Philip Seymour or Pioneer Life in Richland County Founded on Facts* (Mansfield, 1858), 5–6, 22-23, 46, 112.

sometimes able to avert trouble between the Indians and the white settlers. Completely free of race consciousness, he understood the viewpoint of both races.

Johnny Appleseed could read the book of Nature as readily as any Indian, and he could clothe his thoughts in language as vividly pictorial as that of any Indian orator. Johnny could understand the symbolism of their religious rites and their ideas of a future life, for he, too, thought in pictures.

During the War of 1812, Johnny Appleseed was ever on the lookout for trouble with the Indians. One of the earliest settlers of the Firelands, Hanson Read, made arrangements with Johnny to come to his house once a week to let him know how things were going in the war. One day in the late summer, Read was out in the woods hunting his cows, when Johnny suddenly appeared in the clearing, shouting, "Fly for your lives, the Canadians and Indians are landing at Huron!"

The Reads packed up immediately, hid their iron ware and some of their most valuable things in the woods, took Mrs. Read and her young baby with some bedding and other necessities on a sled and started for the blockhouse at Mansfield.

Johnny continued on, stopping at every cabin door to warn of danger. However, it turned out that the British and the Indians were not coming, after all. Johnny had seen a large number of General Hull's soldiers, who had been captured and robbed of their clothing and arms, landing at Huron. They had been sent back by the British in a destitute condition, each soldier wrapped in a blanket provided by his captors.

The Reads lived in one of the blockhouses until January, Mr. Read working in a brickyard. One night he failed to return at the usual time. The people became much alarmed, and a report came in that Read had been scalped. After a while, Read came in unharmed, to tell that a man named Jones, a storekeeper, had been murdered a short distance from town. The villagers fled to the blockhouses, and Johnny Appleseed volunteered to go to Mount Vernon, twenty-six miles away, for help. Johnny ran through the night, over a new-cut road, stopping at each lonely cabin to warn against the Indians.[4] When he reached Mount Vernon, Captain William Douglas mustered as many of his men as he could and left orders for the rest to follow. He took up the line of march about three o'clock in the morning and reached Mansfield about ten o'clock with Johnny and the troops. When Johnny was asked how he accomplished the feat of bringing help so quickly, he replied that God gives the strength for the appointed task.[*]

After the excitement of the war had died down, Johnny Appleseed worked his way over into the Maumee Valley. A treaty was made at the foot of the Maumee Rapids, in 1817, by which a large tract of land in the Maumee Valley was ceded to the United States. The land was but a wilderness, with no improvements other than those made by the Indians. As the Indians removed westward, settlers appropriated the deserted cabins and lived in them until they could make their own improvements. Many settlers lived in an Indian hut when they first came to the new lands in Ohio

[*]Frank D. Read, "Pioneer Life in Huron County," *Firelands Pioneer* V, 126; Col. Edward Wheeler, "Firelands Reminiscences," *Firelands Pioneer* II, 37; M'Gaw, *Philip Seymour,* 108; A. J. Baughman, "Johnny Appleseed," *Ohio State Arch. and Hist. Pub.,* IX 309.

and lived as primitively as did Johnny Appleseed. The "New Purchase" was slow to attract settlers, but Johnny went ahead to plant for the market that would surely develop.

Johnny Appleseed was often seen around St. Mary's. He stayed all night with the family of Samuel Scott on their "Old Town" farm west of St. Mary's, on an average of twice a year. Scott said that, in winter, Johnny wore cast-off shoes, tied on with many-colored strings wound around his ankles in all directions, but that in summer he went barefoot. He sometimes wore one shoe only, breaking the snow with the shod foot. He was known in the Maumee Valley as something of a philosopher, a Swedenborgian, and a dispenser of books. Once a year, he came through to see about his nurseries, continuing on his way to inspect his apple trees on the Auglaize and the Maumee, all the way to Lake Erie.[*]

He started a nursery about one mile above Defiance about 1828, at the mouth of the Tiffin River. Defiance was then a town only six years old. It had been an important trading post between the Canadian French and Indians. Johnny planted a nursery of several thousand trees, taking up later to reset on a more favorable tract of land. There they remained until a resident agent sold them out. Most of the early orchards on the Maumee and Auglaize bottoms in Defiance, Paulding, and Henry Counties are said to have been started from Johnny's nursery near Defiance.[†]

Local records show and traditions indicate that John Chapman had nurseries in Ashland, Auglaize, Champaign,

---

[*]Wm. F. McMurray, *History of Auglaize County, Ohio* (2 vols., Indianapolis, 1923), I, 535.

[†]*History of Defiance County, Ohio* (Chicago, 1883), 109–110; J. D. Simkins, *Early History of Auglaize County* (St. Mary's, 1901), 70–71; Howe, *Collections*, 539, 541–542. For pioneer life of this region, see H. S. Knapp, *History of the Maumee Valley* (Toledo, 1872).

Coshocton, Clark, Crawford, Defiance, Delaware, Guernsey, Hancock, Huron, Jefferson, Knox, Licking, and Logan Counties. The construction of the Miami Canal was recommended in 1824, and it was actually begun in Middletown, Ohio, in 1825. It would have been a natural procedure, on Johnny's part, to plant nurseries all along the proposed route of the canal to Toledo. Other counties that claim Johnny Appleseed nurseries are Butler, Carroll, Harrison, Mercer, and Warren.

Johnny Appleseed occasionally visited Swedenborgian families in Cincinnati, in Hamilton County. Among these families was the Eckstein family. Mrs. Jane Eckstein was the daughter of Francis Bailey of Philadelphia who was the first publisher of Swedenborg's works in America and the first New Churchman in America. Bailey died in 1817, and his widow with a son and three daughters removed to Cincinnati the next year. Jane Bailey Eckstein and her husband came to Cincinnati a few years later to take charge of the school established by the Misses Bailey.

Francis Bailey's youngest daughter, Abbe, married John H. James of Cincinnati, and the young couple removed to Urbana, Ohio, to make their home. In 1826, Alexander Kinmont, a New Churchman who had married Mrs. James's niece, sent John Chapman to John H. James for legal advice concerning a nursery in Champaign County. Johnny Appleseed had planted the nursery with the permission of a certain landholder. Now that the land had been sold, he wanted to know if the new owner could dispossess him of his trees. He did not seem particularly anxious about the trees, however. He walked to and fro as he talked, eating nuts all the time. James invited him to go home with him to meet his wife and her sister Miss Bailey, but he modestly declined, feeling that he was not properly attired to meet the daughters of Francis Bailey.

New Church records show that Johnny Appleseed had traveled as far north as Detroit by 1821. According to an old document found in the Mercer County courthouse, John Chapman went out to Fort Wayne, Indiana, to make his home in 1828, after he had established his nurseries along the Maumee and the Auglaize. One autumn day in 1830, a citizen of Fort Wayne saw him seated in a section of a hollow tree loaded with apple seeds fresh from the cider presses of the Maumee settlements, landing at Wayne's Fort at the foot of Main Street. The seeds were wet from washing them free of pumice, and the improvised boat was covered with mud and tree moss.[*]

It is said that Johnny planted nurseries at the headwaters of the Illinois River in Grundy County, and New Church records show that he was in Illinois in the 1830s. At that time, there was a revival of land sales in that state. After the Land Law of 1820, it was possible to secure an eighty-acre farm for $100 in cash. It seems entirely possible that Johnny might have followed the portage paths from the Maumee to the Kankakee River to establish nurseries in the new lands then being sold to prospective settlers.

That Chapman made a trip to Iowa in the fall of 1843 is stated by Silas Mitchell, who at that time was living in Whiteside County, Illinois. Johnny passed through Whiteside County on foot and stopped at the home of a friend to stay all night. He said that he had been to Iowa and that he was on his way to Philadelphia to a New Church

---

[*] *Indiana Historical Bulletin* XII, 76; Ft. Wayne Johnny Appleseed Memorial Commission booklet.

convention.* After the close of the Black Hawk War, the fifty-mile strip known as the Black Hawk Purchase was quickly settled. By the time that Johnny Appleseed went there, the Indian title to the lands had been extinguished, releasing to settlement the fertile Des Moines Valley, and immigrants were swarming into the Purchase and into the Indian lands beyond the legal boundary.† Chapman is said to have gone into southern Michigan to Holland, Cassopolis, and St. Joseph.

In the Midwest, there are many stories of Johnny Appleseed. Johnny always takes on the trappings of the local folk hero, and often becomes attached to some local event of importance. In Kentucky, they will tell you that he knew Abraham Lincoln and John James Audubon, and that his sweetheart died in Owensboro on the eve of their wedding. In Missouri, they will tell you that he married an Indian girl, and that he warned a French refugee against the Indians, saying

> I sow while others reap
>
> Be sure my warnings keep
>
> Indians will come by break of day
>
> Indians hunting scalps, I say.‡

In Missouri folklore, he is a fiddler and singer of ballads. He may have sung ballads, but it is hard to imagine him

---

*A. Banning Norton, *A History of Knox County, Ohio* (Columbus, 1962), 50. This must have been in the fall of 1842, for the General Convention met in Philadelphia in June 1843.
†Clark, 187–188.
‡Iantha Castlio, "A Folk Tale of Johnny Appleseed," *Missouri Historical Review* XIX, 622–629.

carrying a fiddle in a bag that could have held apple seeds and the writings of Swedenborg. It is equally difficult to think of him singing in a public square and taking alms from a fortuitous audience.

From Johnny's contemporaries, we are able to gain some idea of his personal appearance. He is described as small and wiry, of average height, quick in speech, and restless in motion. His cheeks were hollow and his body spare because he walked so much and ate so little. His face and neck were bronzed and lined by wind and sun. He had extraordinarily brilliant eyes, dark and piercing. He had a well-shaped head and wore his long, black hair parted in the middle and tucked behind his ears to fall about his neck and shoulders. His hair was fine and glossy. A coal-black beard, lightly set and carelessly groomed, gave him a somewhat vagabond look. He never used a razor but sometimes trimmed his beard with a pair of scissors. He was not handsome, surely, but there was something compelling in those deep-set burning eyes.

He possessed a peculiar eloquence, too. He could hold an apple in his hand and discourse so charmingly upon that fruit that it became a thing of exquisite beauty and delight. He is said to have had a resonant voice that could be persuasively tender, inspirationally sublime, or witheringly denunciatory. He possessed a keen sense of humor, quick to make a witty retort or a cutting rebuke. He was sincerely patriotic, too. He had unlimited faith in his country. On one occasion, at least, he made a Fourth of July oration—at a celebration in the cabin of Levi Cole in Huron County.*

---

*Martin Kellogg, *Norwalk Reflector*, June 25, 1883.

Johnny may not have been well-dressed, even by frontier standards. He is pictured as wearing a buttonless shirt,
open to wind and sun and rain and snow, bloused over to
form a pocket for his Bible. His trousers were short and
frazzled at the bottom from briars and burrs, and were sup-
ported in a half-hearted fashion by some original substitute
for suspenders. Much has been written about the tow-linen
coffee sack he wore for a coat and the tin pot he wore upon
his head. The latter would be simply a matter of efficiency.
To one who had to sustain life and earn a living with what
he carried upon his back, it was only natural to make one
thing take the place of two. Obviously, he could not make
mush in a hat or cap. Sometimes he wore a crownless hat,
which, if he chose, he could carry on his arm. Again, he
might be seen wearing an old revolutionary soldier's hat,
sometimes with tracts snugly anchored beneath its crown.
In short, he wore on his head whatever was convenient. As
for the tow-linen coat, with a hole cut for his head, that was
not so unusual. Many a circuit-rider cut a hole in a blanket,
pulled it over his head, and wore it for a coat. Fastidious
theater-goers of early Cincinnati complained because gentle-
men from Kentucky attended the play in blankets rather
than coats. Salathiel Coffinberry, who knew Johnny well,
said that Johnny's coat was not a coffee sack, that it was "a
kind of long-tailed coat of tow-linen then much worn by
farmers." Johnny designed the coat himself. It consisted of
one width of the coarse fabric, which reached from his
shoulders to his heels. Coffinberry's mother made it for
Johnny under his immediate supervision, cutting the two
armholes and setting in a pair of straight sleeves.[*]

---

[*]Brinkerhoff Scrapbook, Clipping No. 22.

Aside from the scantiness of his attire, Johnny dressed much as other men in the more remote settlements. Both men and women went barefooted in summer, although they wore moccasins or shoe packs in winter to keep out the cold. It was said that he could walk over the ice and snow barefooted in the coldest weather and never feel it. The skin was so thick on his feet that one of his acquaintances said it would kill a rattlesnake to try to bite Johnny's feet. He was peculiarly insensitive to pain. He could sear a wound with a red-hot poker and never flinch. He learned from the Indians to sear a wound and treat it as a burn. The common dress of the frontiersman in 1800 was a pair of dressed deerskin or blue cloth pantaloons, a blue handkerchief tied over the head, deerskin moccasins on the feet, and a blanket coat tied round the waist with a belt. From one side of the belt was suspended a pouch of dressed polecat skin to hold tobacco, pipe, flint, and steel. Under the belt on the other side a butcher knife was carried.* A blue linsey hunting shirt with a belt fringed in gay colors was considered very fine. In summer, farmers wore long-tailed tow-linen shirts, something like a peasant's smock. As to poverty of purse, Johnny probably had more money in his pocket than many a settler, and more than most itinerant preachers, who received from twenty-eight to one hundred dollars a year.

As for Johnny's diet, it was a little more frugal than that of many of the pioneer Methodist circuit-riders. They carried jerked meat and journey bread for their food. Johnny ate nuts and fruits in their season, made mush in his tin pot, or ate sparingly of a bit of food given him by some generous housewife. He would not eat meat because he

---

*History of Wayne County, Indiana, I, 369.

thought it wrong to destroy life. Johnny must have carried journey bread at times. That was a standard traveling food among the Indians. It was so highly nutritious and portable that the soldiers in the War of 1812 were advised to carry it with them on their marches. Notices were published in the newspapers with full directions for its preparation. It was made by boiling green corn in the roasting ear until half done, drying it in the sun for a few days, browning it in hot ashes, pounding it fine, and finally mixing it with maple sugar.

In his pack, Johnny sometimes carried a present of tea for some housewife who needed a bit of cheer, although he never drank tea himself. He carried a piece of bright calico or a gay ribbon for a child who had saved apple seeds for him during the winter. Children never laughed at Johnny Appleseed. He was their friend. He could tell the most engaging stories; he could whistle and sing the gayest tunes; he could care for a childish hurt in the tenderest way. The little folk trotted at his heels and helped to plant his seeds or care for his young seedlings. As they worked together, Johnny told them of the beautiful land of the New Jerusalem, dropping seeds of truth into young and tender hearts that bore fruit in after years. He told them of the glorious future of the brave new nation they must help to build—a land of opportunity for all. Johnny helped the men with their work and told the news from other settlements. One farmer said that Johnny was the best hand to shuck corn he ever had. Another said that Johnny could split as many rails and girdle as many trees in one day as most men did in two. Johnny was no beggar.

Around Fort Wayne, John Chapman bought up tracts of land amounting to 214½ acres in Allen and Jay

Counties. There are traditions that he owned land in Mount Vernon, Mansfield, and the present town of Lakefork in Ohio, at various times, before he went to Indiana.[5] For many years, Johnny planted and tended his nurseries along the main highways—the rivers and the canals. On the north bank of the Maumee River in Milan Township, he owned a nursery of fifteen-thousand apple trees. He became a familiar figure on the streets of Fort Wayne. In his later years, when strength was failing, he walked beside an old gray horse that he hitched to a cart to draw his load of trees or seeds.[*] Johnny never rode a horse. He would not allow it to do for him what he could do for himself. In the Mohican country, he had been noted for his tenderness toward mistreated and worn-out horses. He bought them up and arranged for their care until he could find good homes for them. He was never known to sell a horse.

Johnny's half-sister, Persis Chapman Broome, lived near Fort Wayne, and it is thought that he lived with or near her at times.[6] Her husband helped him with his nurseries. It was near the home of Persis Broome that Johnny apparently intended to make a permanent home. On this tract in Jay County, he had a nursery of two-thousand trees. On it, at the time of his death, there was already a log cabin, timber dressed and cut for a barn, and eleven acres cleared and fenced. The improvement on the land was done by William Broome.[†]

In 1842, Johnny made his last trip back to Ohio. While there, he made his headquarters at the home of Nathaniel, the brother who had accompanied him to

---

[*]Robert C. Harris, *Lawn Care*, Feb., 1935.
[†]Estate Papers of John Chapman, Allen County, Indiana.

Pennsylvania so long ago. Upon his return to Fort Wayne, he resumed his work as "a gatherer and planter of apple-seeds." On March 18, 1845, he died of pneumonia in the home of his old Richland County friend, William Worth. At the sawmill of Christian Parker, a plain walnut coffin was made for Johnny, and he was buried by his friends in a burial plot not far from Fort Wayne.*

The place of Johnny Appleseed's burial is a controversial subject. Some claim that he was buried in David Archer's graveyard, and others say that he was buried on the Roebuck farm. According to a letter written by Dr. T. N. M'Gaw to Judge Brinkeroff, Richard Worth told M'Gaw:

> We buried him respectably in David Archer's graveyard two and a half miles north of Fort Wayne, he having died at my father's house which to him was a comfortable and welcome home in his old age.†

John Chapman lived in complete harmony with nature. In field and meadow and forest he walked, concerned with the spacious thoughts of God. In his earthly life, he was a one-man circulating library, a one-man humane society, a one-man clinic, a one-man missionary band, and a one-man emigrant-aid society. Johnny Appleseed did not need to die to find heaven, for heaven was in his heart.

Fort Wayne Sentinel, March 22, 1845; Rosa A. Langtry, "A Visit to the Grave of Johnny Appleseed," *Indiana History Bulletin* IV, 218–220; Wesley S. Roebuck, "Outline of Facts Related to the Burial Place of John Chapman," *Ohio Arch. and Hist. Quar.* LII, 275–284. See Price, "References to Death, Burial Place and Estate" in *John Chapman: A Bibliography of "Johnny Appleseed" in American History, Literature and Folklore* (Patterson, N.J.: Swedenborg Press, 1944), 11–13.

†See letter in Brinkerhoff Scrapbook, Clipping No. 20. The letter is dated Norristown, Indiana, June 13, 1858.

Editor's Update

1. In Robert Price's later book *Johnny Appleseed, Man and Myth,* he states on page 16 that John's father, Nathaniel, along with other Springfield officers, was released in late 1780 because of "unsatisfactory management of the company stores." It appears now, however, that Price misinterpreted what limited records were available to him at the time and that Chapman's father has been exonerated.

In an unpublished manuscript, "Let's Put the Record Straight," which was an offshoot of formal documentation prepared for and filed with the Massachusetts Society of the Cincinnati, George B. Huff, FACG, has cleared his ancestor Nathaniel Chapman's name. The following is excerpted with permission by Mr. Huff:

> The Springfield Armory came into existence as General Washington and his staff felt the urgent need for an additional artillery regiment in 1776. . . . Major Joseph Eayre was ordered to command a company of Artillery Artificers at Springfield in January 1777. . . . Nathaniel Chapman, on March 19, 1777, was assigned as Captain of Wheelwrights at Springfield, pursuant to appropriate action by Colonel Henry Knox and/or a warrant of the Board of War, where he remained until September 30, 1780. Perhaps as a reward for good service or perhaps to clarify his commissioned status with the Massachusetts troops, Congress, on 7 May 1778, passed a Resolve, "That the Board of War having recommended Nathaniel Chapman, Esq. to be captain of the additional company to Colonel Flower's regiment of Artillery artificers." The successful conduct of the war where it began in the north had by the Fall of 1779 moved the scene of combat to the south which made a marked effect on the efficiency of the Springfield operation to transport their manufactured, refurbished and restored equipment to the combat troops so far away in the south. This had an interesting effect on their entire supply system for the type of munitions Springfield produced that

caused the Board of War to consider "derangement" or demobilization as a practical method of closing down the Springfield post. *The Journals of the Congress,* Volume XVII, 1780, show concerns for the lessening utility of the armory and began a reduction in force by excusing a number of personnel from further service at that post. Later, on August 26, 1780, Congress passed a Resolve, "That Major Joseph Eayre and Captain Nathaniel Chapman, who have been employed at Springfield in the department of the Commissary-General of the military stores; be excused from further service." The Board of War went further to report that Captain Chapman (and others) be entitled to one year's pay and subsistence.

2. Traditions based on recollections of Judge Lansing Wetmore, an early chronicler of Warren County, Pennsylvania, have John and perhaps his half-brother Nathaniel arriving near Warren in the middle of an early November 1797 snowstorm. The earliest known written record of John Chapman's having been in Pennsylvania is found in John Daniel's store ledger. It was discovered in the early 1950s and contains six entries on page 39 regarding Chapman's purchases in Warren, interpreted by some to have begun on February 14, 1797, and ended on May 3, 1799. Further, six other entries on page 121 include what are believed to be his half-brother Nathaniel's transactions, from June 26 to November 12, 1798.

3. The earliest known reference to Chapman's having possibly been introduced to the Swedenborgian faith is reported in Carl Theophilus Odhner's *Annals of the New Church* (Bryn Athyn, Penna.: 1904). New Church tradition claims Chapman's first contact was through Judge John Young, while in Greensburg, Westmoreland County, Pennsylvania, although this association has not been proved. Young, a close member of Francis Bailey's Swedenborg reading circle in Philadelphia, moved his law practice to Greensburg in 1790, where he continued to introduce the doctrines and distribute Swedenborg publications.

4. *The Ohio Register*, Clinton, Ohio, August 10, 1813, was first to report Johnny Appleseed's run:

> Tuesday Evening, 10th Inst. An express arrived at this place from Mansfield, which place he had left at sunset—stated that the Indians had attacked that Town killed and scalped a Mr. Jones—several men were missing. A number of mounted men from Clinton and vicinity [Mount Vernon] have gone to their assistance.

Now, for the first time, confirmation of this incident and its date can be set with confidence. Witnesses to the affair identified Chapman as the messenger and one claimed, "It was the brightest moon that night I ever saw." Lunar tables have been checked and, indeed, the night of August 9–10, 1813, enjoyed a full moon. Once again, it seems that the right man for the job was available at the right time and that the hand of Providence illuminated the way.

At the time of Johnny's run, Mansfield's Square was the site of two blockhouses erected during the War of 1812 and very few other structures. One blockhouse, constructed of round logs by a Captain Schaeffer of Fairfield County, Ohio, stood at the intersection of Main and Park Avenue West. Colonel Charles Williams of Coshocton County, Ohio, built the other blockhouse of hewn logs. It was located in the middle of the north side of the square and soon served as Mansfield's first courthouse. The settlements of Clinton and Mount Vernon, Ohio, were in close proximity to each other and located about twenty-six miles south of Mansfield.

5. These traditions have been confirmed in land records of Richland and Ashland Counties, as have others in Ohio counties. His first known recorded property consisted of two town lots in Mount Vernon, Ohio, which he purchased for $50 on September 14, 1809 (Knox County Deeds A, 116). It has been estimated

that Chapman likely held deeds to almost 1,200 acres of land at various times throughout his lifetime.

6. According to early records of Green Township, Ashland County, Ohio, Persis and William Broom lived near Perrysville from about 1816 to 1830 and just west of Mansfield, Ohio, on the old Leesville Road (500 West Fourth Street) from about 1830 to 1835, after which it is believed they moved to Jay County, Indiana.

New Information
About an Old Friend

by William Ellery Jones

ortunately, for historians and students of Americana, the 1940s through the mid-1950s experienced a blizzard of information and activity surrounding John Chapman. Leominster, Massachusetts, celebrated its bicentennial in 1940 and dedicated a granite marker at the traditional site of Appleseed's birthplace. Leominster librarian Florence Wheeler had just finished her Chapman family genealogy the year before and established Appleseed's birth date as September 26, 1774. A monument at the site of the Chapman family's later residence near Dexter City, Ohio, was dedicated in 1942. Another researcher, Anna Long Onstott, who lived in Mansfield, Ohio (referenced in this book's footnotes under Ophia Smith's chapter) was trying to complete the first serious work on Johnny Appleseed. Unfortunately, she died before finishing her project, but Onstott did lecture and publish some shorter articles in magazines. Her most complete effort was co-written with

Arthur N. Stunz, "John Chapman—Johnny Appleseed," which was published in the *Men's Garden Clubs of America Year Book*, 1943. The one-hundred-year commemoration of Chapman's death (1945) was marked by the Swedenborg Press's publishing Robert Price's *John Chapman: A Bibliography* (1944) and the first edition of the book you are now reading, *Johnny Appleseed: A Voice in the Wilderness* (1945). Also, in 1945, Robert C. Harris, inventor, long-time Indiana teacher and high-school principal published his *Johnny Appleseed Source Book*, which appeared as volume IX of the Allen county–Fort Wayne Historical Society's "Old Fort News." It contained an organized presentation of Chapman's estate papers and local traditions leading up to his death. Controversy over the authentic site of Chapman's grave was partially settled in 1949, when the Fort Wayne Common Council passed an ordinance identifying the site within Johnny Appleseed Memorial Park. Johnny Appleseed Memorial Bridge was also dedicated in Fort Wayne the same year.

In 1948, Walt Disney released his animated film *Melody Time*, a musical anthology of American folk heroes that included Johnny Appleseed and the versatile voice of Dennis Day as Appleseed, narrator and guardian angel. Disney must be credited for the popular image of the scrawny, carefree, mushpot-hat-clad Appleseed that exists in the minds of many today. This cartoon characterization opened the floodgates to countless children's books thereafter, such as Mabel Leigh Hunt's *Better Known as Johnny Appleseed* in 1950. In 1953, H. Kenneth Dirlam, a banker from Mansfield, Ohio, published "John Chapman, by Occupation a Gatherer and Planter of Appleseeds," a valuable compilation of mainly regional Johnny Appleseed folklore and traditions. In conjunction with the reorganization of the Richland

County Historical Society and its celebration of Ohio's sesquicentennial on September 26, 1953, renown Johnny Appleseed experts Dirlam, Price, Harris, and Wheeler converged in Mansfield for festivities that included dedication of a new Johnny Appleseed monument that replaced one originally erected in 1900.

Since these events and Robert Price's monumental book *Johnny Appleseed: Man and Myth*, published in 1954, no other "major" historical work has been offered. However, when one exhausts biographical information about a subject, often one can still learn more by studying the lives of those with whom the subject was involved. Many new bits of information can be found in the "Editor's Update" at the end of each of the original chapters in this book. In themselves, these recently uncovered facts probably don't alter history, but they do provide interest and enlightenment to those who would like to know more about this unique individual. Let's consider some.

A Case for Nursery Island

For many Appleseed enthusiasts, the prospect of identifying an Appleseed nursery site is enthralling. One in particular is especially enchanting.

There are probably few more romantic spots in Ohio than the lower branch of the Mohican River where its heavily wooded high walls meet the Kokosing (Owl Creek) in Knox and Coshocton Counties to form the Walhounding (White Woman's Creek). Here, possibly as early as 1801, John Chapman began establishing several nurseries in Coshocton county—one in New Castle township and two in close proximity to each other in Tiverton township. The third location was known widely as Nursery Island and referenced in N.N. Hill's *History of Knox County, Ohio*, page 435, as being in the Mohican River, a short distance from the line between Butler Township, Knox County and Coshocton County. Robert Price's *Johnny Appleseed: Man and Myth*, page 66, states that "the location is uncertain now. From it came many a fine tree." Based on Hill's description, obtained from those who remembered it, and my personal interviews, I believe, without question, I can prove that the island still exists!

In one of only four known communications in Chapman's own handwriting, John Butler is referenced. It reads: "October 1812. For value received I promise to pay or cause to be paid to Benjamin Burrel one hundred and fifty trees at my nursery near John Butler's in the month of March such as they are when called for. John Chapman." The order was most recently owned by the Johnny Appleseed District, Boy Scouts of America, in Mansfield, Ohio, and is believed to have been consumed in an office fire in the 1960s.

The Butler family arrived early and played a prominent role in the settling of Mount Vernon, the lower Mohican River and Owl Creek valleys. John Butler owned property situated just west and over the hill from Nursery Island. Although some Burrells lived in Coshocton County at the time, they also were referenced in early Richland County history and carried quite a reputation for weekend brawls between the Black forkers and the Clear forkers who settled on tributaries of the Mohican. Chapman traveled extensively and often utilized neighbors as agents to tend his nurseries and assist in business transactions. Since seedlings were said to have been obtained from this area at an early date, it is supposed that "Mohican Waters" were a mainstay for Appleseed's nursery business for many years.

A current U. S. Geological Survey topographic map shows that this same island is identical to one depicted in an original survey from 1837 for an extension of the Walhounding Canal from Roscoe Village to Rochester (Cavallo), Ohio. The location, shape, and form of both islands are identical and match, perfectly, the one that still exists today. Also, a map in the field notebook for the original land survey conducted by William Rufus Putnam in 1805 appears to indicate the same island in the same place. Today, the island is still remote and is situated three-tenths of a mile north of the old "Wally" railroad trestle (dismantled in November 1993). It is owned by the Ohio Department of Natural Resources.

Using the Legal System

While perusing through old documents in the Knox County (Ohio) courthouse, I discovered that Chapman had filed suit against James Craig. The case is listed in the minutes from the court of common pleas; 1808–1816; Vol. A; p. 5A; January 1813; "Chapman, John vs. Craig, James [p.] 86." Disposition: "dismissed other costs of/by plaintiff."

Craig was widely known for his raucous behavior and readiness to engage in brawls. What this particular conflict involved is not known, but, evidently, Chapman changed his mind about it. Still, the fact that John Chapman was using the legal system shows that he was not one to just cower away from every impropriety with which he was confronted.

Further research uncovered that Chapman was, in turn, named as one of four defendants in a separate lawsuit in Knox County, August 4, 1813. It seems Josiah Hedges, (who would later found Tiffin, Ohio) was owed a note for $150 from Samuel Kratzer, Andrew Craig, George Davis, and John Chapman. For some unknown reason, Chapman's name was dropped from the case before it was settled for $200 at the Knox County Supreme Court's sixth term in 1815. Hedges was a brother of General James Hedges, who surveyed much of original Richland County, Ohio, in 1806 and laid out the town of Tiffin for Josiah in 1821. About the time of this lawsuit, Josiah joined his brother's mercantile business in Mansfield. Kratzer helped settle Mount Vernon, was a colonel in the Ohio militia during the War of 1812, and was responsible for giving orders to remove the Delaware Indians from their village of Greentown (near Perrysville, Ohio). This latter situation eventually led to Indians' attacking the Copus family on the Blackfork, September 15, 1812, and to traditions of Johnny Appleseed's spreading news of the incident. Craig was the first permanent white settler in Knox County, the man upon whose camp Chapman planted an early nursery. Both Craig and Kratzer play major roles in the Johnny Appleseed Outdoor Drama, scheduled to open June 2000 at the Johnny Appleseed Heritage Center, in Johnny Appleseed Forest, near Mansfield, Ohio.

Rosella Rice

Rosella Rice was a third-generation original settler in Perrysville, Ohio, where Johnny Appleseed had a cabin in the second decade of the 1800s. She was eighteen years of age when Chapman died in 1845. The Rice family may have let Chapman use their old original cabin built in 1811, following construction of their improved habitation, or he may have erected a crude poll cabin on the Rice farm for himself. His half-sister Persis Broom and her husband William (from Marietta, Ohio) lived a mile or so northeast of the Rice property on what later became known as the Cowan farm. Chapman's brother-in-law, William Broom, was tending to John's local nurseries while Chapman traveled elsewhere. By this time, Chapman had numerous documented nurseries along the Blackfork River, all within a day's canoe ride.

Arthur's Ladies Home Magazine, volume 44 (c.1876), page 15, included Rosella's recollection about her visit to the site of the locally famous Copus massacre, which transpired during the War of 1812, five miles north of Rosella's home. Rosella's story was published just five years before she recommended to a Copus monument committee in 1882 that Johnny Appleseed's name be included on the obelisk; making the Copus/Appleseed monument the first, hence, oldest known monument to Johnny Appleseed's memory erected anywhere in the world.

A later resident of the original Rice farm remembers, as a child, being left to babysit her younger brothers and sisters while her parents went for groceries in Perrysville, a short distance down the hill. In the parents' absence, she and her siblings were forbidden to climb a ladder that accessed the attic. Naturally, as soon as the parents were out of sight, all of the children ascended the rickety contraption and discovered boxes of Rosella's papers, manuscripts, and letters. One very old envelope in particular caught her eye—a letter from John Chapman, Fort Wayne, Indiana, to Rosella Rice, Perrysville, Ohio. Rosella, no doubt, was a favorite of Chapman, as he returned to the area annually to pay taxes, visit friends, and gather seed, possibly up to the year just before his death. The former resident did not remember the letter's content or date; but she did report that, as she and her family were pulling out of the driveway to their new quarters, house cleaners were seen pitching papers and other items from the upstairs window to a hungry trash fire below, which was already consuming countless unidentified gems of Rosella Rice's written history.

In one of Rice's obituaries written by a relative, Mary O. Eddy (who later published *Ballads and Songs from Ohio*, many of which were collected in and around Perrysville) stated that, at her death (1888), Rosella was working on Johnny Appleseed's biography. The manuscript has never been found.

Bill Collector or Mailman?

Following the War of 1812, two Indian reservations were set up at Upper Sandusky for each tribe of Wyandotts and Delawares. By 1826, the Delaware were scheduled, once again, to be removed to Kansas and elsewhere. Although this diaspora did not happen until 1829, some merchants attempted to collect on past bills. It appears that Chapman delivered several past-due invoices for a storekeeper in Mansfield to at least two Delaware Indians, Solomon Johnnacake and Billy Dowdee, whom he knew from earlier years at Greentown. One note reads, "The bearer Mr. John Chapman has taken some accounts on the late firm of Sturgis & Sherwood, from the Delaware & Windot [sic] , Indians, to collect, the agent will much oblige the subscriber. He will like this account settled. E.B. Sturges." Another, "Friend Johnacake be so good as to pay this above to bearer & oblige your Sturgis & Sherwood." Johnnacake was well liked by the settlers and continued to hunt around his old neighborhood of Greentown for many years. He was one of the last to leave Upper Sandusky. Chapman and Johnnacake had likely known each other since the early 1800s, and John would have stopped at the Upper Sandusky reservation often, during his western Ohio operations.

Missionary Zeal

Evidently, John Chapman was still active with his self-imposed missionary work later in life. He died on March 18, 1845. His obituary, published in the Fort Wayne *Sentinel* on March 22, 1845, states that "He was a devout follower of Swedenborgh [sic]. . . We understand his home—if home he had—for some years past was in the neighborhood of Cleveland, Ohio, where he has relatives living." An area west of Cleveland was known as Rockport (which later became Lakewood), where there lived a strong following of Swedenborg readers. Among them were the Wagars, whose family traditions recall visits by Johnny Appleseed. Francis Wagar married Serena Tucker, daughter of John Tucker from Richland County, Ohio. John Tucker, who helped his brother lay out the town of Lucas, Ohio, and lead a group of Swedenborg readers near there, was introduced to the faith by John Chapman and concluded that Johnny's tracts contained as much religion as any man needed. Tucker even used the same route as Johnny Appleseed when he made a trip by foot to Fort Wayne in 1828.

Chapman sold one of his land holdings in Plain Township, Wayne County, to John H. Pile, on September 8,

1832, for $50. Pile was a Swedenborgian who assisted Reverend H. N. Strong in developing a group of readers near Wooster, Ohio. Strong later lived and preached in Savannah, Ohio, not far from Martin Mason's mill, where Chapman maintained a long-standing nursery. Also, Reverend Strong succeeded Silas Ensign, who earlier, some believe, had been introduced to the Swedenborgian faith by John Chapman in Richland County and who had been recommended by John to the church for ordination. Ensign later changed his mind and reverted back to his Methodist faith.

In Cincinnati, the Eckstein and Kinmont families also spoke of Johnny Appleseed's visits. John H. James reported that Chapman visited him in Urbana with a letter of introduction from Alexander Kinmont in 1826. Kinmont arrived in America from Scotland in 1823; spent three years in Bedford, Pennsylvania; was introduced to the Swedenborgian faith there; and didn't move to Cincinnati until 1827. While in Bedford, he did, however make one round trip, on foot, to Cincinnati before relocating. It seems likely that Chapman and Kinmont would have met in the Bedford area or on the trail in Ohio during Kinmont's first visit to Cincinnati. The scene of both men contemplating Swedenborg over a shared campfire in the Ohio wilderness would certainly have warranted recording. Later, in Cincinnati, Kinmont became a great orator, a leader in the Swedenborgian church, and wrote his highly acclaimed *Twelve Lectures on the Natural History of Man*, shortly before his untimely death in 1838. His brother William owned land in Richland County near John Tucker in the 1820s and also was a member of a Swedenborgian congregation. He and his family moved to Cincinnati before Alexander's death, but eventually settled in Tiffin, Ohio.

Johnny's Burial

The battle over where John Chapman is buried in Fort Wayne, Indiana, ensued for many years between two factions, one favoring Swinney Park (or the old Roebuck farm) and the other the Archer cemetery. The issue may have been settled, however, in 1978. That year, Steven Fortriede, associate director of the Fort Wayne and Allen County Public Library, published *Johnny Appleseed: The Man Behind the Myth*, which asserted,

> [W]e can state in conclusion that John Chapman, Johnny Appleseed, died at the home of Richard Worth, Senior [not William Worth as previously believed] and that he was buried somewhere in Archer burial ground [located on the west bank of the St. Joseph River]. We voice this conclusion fully realizing the fact, indeed we wish to specifically to point out that, while there exists no definite proof as yet, the preponderance of the evidence and the only documentary evidence available indicates that Richard Worth, Sr., lived on the east bank of the St. Joseph River, on or near the land which later became known as the Roebuck farm.

Members of the same Worth family were reported to have been timber cutters and to have lived in Richland County, Ohio, prior to settling in Fort Wayne.

Johnny Appleseed Memorial Park, which contains Archer burial ground, is the site for Johnny Appleseed Festival, sponsored by the Fort Wayne Parks and Recreation Department and others. Every third weekend in September, over 200,000 visitors converge to relive the folkways of Johnny Appleseed's time.

It is comforting to know that our friend John Chapman was very conscious of the overlapping relationships in both the physical and spiritual worlds and not only cultivated count-less apple trees, but also, countless friends. He still does today.

The American Pioneer

John Chapman—Johnny Appleseed

by John W. Stockwell

John Chapman—"Johnny Appleseed," so named,
Caused wild-sown soil and soul—to be reclaimed
From wilderness; and creeds in darkness framed.
He harmed no living thing. He served the maimed.
The urge of life in slender stalks of grain,
The growth of grass and bushes on the plain,
The shaggy-fronded forest on the hill—
To him were patterns that man's thoughts fulfill:
This tree that finds its way to light above
Is man's response to God's creative love;
From seed and sapling, on its mission sent,
Its outflung branches choir and testament:
It holds itself erect in reverence:
Its apples, rounded poems, rich in redolence,
Are symbols of delight to soul and sense,
For stress of growth a golden recompense.
As Moses saw within a bush the fire
And heard the Voice to noble task inspire.
So Chapman saw in trees the glowing word
Of Deity in growing things; and heard
The inner call to bring, as welcomed guest,
To settlers of America's mid-west
The brightness of the orchard's bloom and fruit

And truth to free from doubting and dispute.

He saw the brute in man but never blamed,

Believing diverse ways are heaven-aimed.

The Christian faith of Swedenborg, far-famed,

His guide, his soul inspired, his self-hood tamed.

The apple seeds and saplings in a pack,

And Bible and his books, upon his back,

While pages of the "wonder book" held high—

"Here's news from heaven," was his cry.

For Swedenborg had written of the scene

In "Heaven," also "Hell" and "World Between."

A revelation from the Lord—rebirth

Made known—His light to guide mankind on earth.

So Chapman left some pages with each call,

And thus his host, perchance might gather all.

Some men of might have hewn great forests clear

And others fought to free our land from fear,

Or marvels of vast industries have wrought.

Such heroes, known, are honored in our thought.

But here is one who felt our nation's needs,

John Chapman—"Johnny Appleseed"—and deeds

Obscure performed. At last the public heeds

The message of the orchard truth that leads

From fruit of flesh to fruit of soul—and seeds

Of faith that flower far above old creeds:

To herald God as Jesus, Lord and King,

And "future life" where reigns eternal spring.

Oh, what a valiant patriot was he

To plant such faith beside the apple tree!

RESOURCE LIST

The following is intended for use by students of the life of Johnny Appleseed, whether the man or the myth. It is selective, rather than comprehensive, although I have tried to include in each category material on what I believe to be the best works or most important site.

The list includes books, films, and other treatments on the life or myth of John "Appleseed" Chapman. With the exception of the Disney film, it does not include the numerous treatments of the man and his legend that have been created for children or young adults. If the actual or mythical figure of Johnny Appleseed appears in only part of a cited work, I have listed the page numbers.

Scholarly Studies

Bibliography

Price, Robert. *John Chapman: A Bibliography of "Johnny Appleseed" in American History, Literature and Folklore.* Patterson, N.J.: Swedenborg Press, 1944.

Historical Studies of John Chapman

Brinkerhoff, Roeliff. *A Pioneer History of Richland County, Ohio.* Edited by Mary Jane Henney. Mansfield, Ohio: Ohio Genealogical Society, Richland County Chapter, 1993.

Dirlam, H. Kenneth. *John Chapman, by Occupation a Gatherer and Planter of Appleseeds.* Mansfield, Ohio: The Richland County Historical Society, 1953.

———. *Bits of History from Talks Here and There.* Mansfield, Ohio: The Richland County Historical Society, 1965, 5–32.

Fortriede, Steven. *Johnny Appleseed: The Man Behind the Myth.* Fort Wayne, Ind.: Fort Wayne Public Library, 1978. Pamphlet.

Glines, W. M. *Johnny Appleseed by One Who Knew Him.* Columbus, Ohio: The F. J. Heer Printing Co., 1922. Pamphlet.

Haley, W. D. "Johnny Appleseed—A Pioneer Hero." *Harper's Monthly Magazine* XLIII (Nov., 1871): 830–836. Reprinted in *Harper's.* Sandwich, Mass.: Chapman Billes, Inc., 1994.

Harris, Robert C., ed. "Johnny Appleseed Source Book." *Old Fort News* (Fort Wayne, Indiana) IX (March–June, 1945): 1–31.

Hatcher, Harlan. *The Buckeye Country.* New York: H. C. Kinsey & Co., Inc., 1940. See pages 166–173.

Howe, Henry. *Historical Collections of Ohio.* Cincinnati: 1847, 1889–1891, 1896. In the last edition, see vol. 1, page 260; and vol. 2, pages 484–487 and 673.

Journal of the Proceedings of the Fifth General Convention of the New Jerusalem. Philadelphia, June 3–5, 1822.

Knapp, H. S. *History of the Pioneer and Modern Times of Ashland County, Ohio.* Philadelphia: 1863. See pages 27–38.

Mather, George R. *Frontier Faith: The Story of the Pioneer Congregations of Fort Wayne, Indiana, 1820–1860.* Fort Wayne, Ind.: The Allen County–Fort Wayne Historical Society, 1992. See pages 235–240.

Norton, A. Banning. *A History of Knox County, Ohio, from 1779 to 1862 Inclusive.* Columbus, Ohio, 1862. See pages 50, 128, 130–135, 140.

Odhner, Carl Theophilus. *Annals of the New Church.* Vol 1. Bryn Athyn, Penna., 1904.

Price, Robert. "A Boyhood for Johnny Appleseed." *New England Quarterly* XVII (Sept., 1944): 381–393.

———. *Johnny Appleseed: Man and Myth.* Bloomington, Ind: Indiana University Press, 1954. Reprinted Gloucester, Mass.: Peter Smith, 1967.

———. "Johnny Appleseed: Yankee Peddler." *Farm Quarterly* V (Summer, 1950): 80–81.

_____. "The Man in the Mushpot Hat." *The New-Church Messenger*, Nov. 15, 1961, 339–341.

_____. "The New England Origins of Johnny Appleseed." *New England Quarterly* XII (Sept., 1939): 454–469.

Report of the Society for Printing, Publishing and Circulating the Writings of Emanuel Swedenborg. Manchester, England, Jan. 14, 1817.

Samuels, Gayle Brandow. *Enduring Roots: Encounters with Trees, History, and the American Lanscape.* New Brunswick, N.J.: Rutgers University Press, 1999. See pages 56–61.

Wheeler, Florence E. "John Chapman." In *Leominster 200th Anniversary.* Leominster, Mass., 1940. See pages 15–17.

_____. "John Chapman's Line of Descent from Edward Chapman of Ipswich." *Ohio Archeological and Historical Quarterly* XLVIII (Jan., 1939): 28–33.

Williams, Gary S. *Johnny Appleseed in the Duck Creek Valley.* Dexter City, Ohio: Johnny Appleseed Center for Creative Learning, 1989. Pamphlet.

Popular Treatments

Fiction

Atkinson, Eleanor. *Johnny Appleseed: The Romance of the Sower.* New York: Harper & Brothers, 1915.

Catherwood, Mary Hartwell. *Lazarre.* Indianapolis, Ind.: Cather & Brothers 1901.

Fast, Howard. *The Tall Hunter.* New York: Harper & Brothers, 1942.

Hillis, Newell Dwight. *The Quest of John Chapman: The Story of a Forgotten Hero.* New York: The Macmillan Co., 1904.

Lindsay, Vachel. *The Golden Book of Springfield, N.Y.* New York: The Macmillan Co., 1920.

_____. *The Litany of Washington Street.* New York: The Macmillan Co., 1929. See pages 69–93.

M'Gaw, James F. *Philip Seymour; or, Pioneer Life in Richland County, Ohio.* Mansfield, Ohio: 1857, 1883, 1902, 1908. 5th edition, Mansfield, Ohio: Little Journeys Bookshop, 1999.

Nonfiction

Botkin, B. A., ed. *A Treasury of American Folklore.* New York: Crown Publishers, 1944; see pages 255–256 and 261–270.
_____. *A Treasury of New England Folklore.* New York: Crown Publishers, 1947. See pages 558–560.
Bromfield, Louis. *The Farm.* New York: Harper & Brothers, 1933. See pages 103–105.
_____. *Pleasant Valley.* New York: Harper & Brothers, 1945. See pages 26–35, 90–91.
Ellis, William Donohue. *With a Name Like . . .* Orrville, Ohio: The J. M, Smucker Company, 1987. See page 10.
Frost, Frances. "Johnny Appleseed." In *Legends of the United Nations.* New York: 1943. See pages 154–161.

Poetry

Benét, Rosemary and Stephen Vincent. "Johnny Appleseed." In *A Book of Americans.* New York: Farrar and Rinehart, Inc., 1933. See pages 47–49.
Child, Lydia Maria. "Apple-Seed John." *St. Nicholas* VII (July, 1880): 604–605.
Crawford, Joshua. "Billy Stevens or Life on the Mohicans." In *1812.* Columbus, Ohio: The F. J. Heer Printing Co., 1918. See pages 100–101.
Frost, Frances. "American Ghost." In *New York Herald Tribune,* Aug. 21, 1943.
Leverenz, Ernest C. *Johnny Appleseed and Shorter Poems.* New York: The Exposition Press, 1951.
Lindsay, Vachel. "In Praise of Johnny Appleseed" and eight other poems on the same theme. In *Collected Poems.* New York: The Macmillan Co., 1927.

———. "The Apple-Barrel of Johnny Appleseed" and "Johnny Appleseed Still Farther West." In *Going to the Sun*. New York: D. Appleton and Company, 1923.

———. *Johnny Appleseed and Other Poems*. New York: The Macmillan Co., 1928, 1930.

Masters, Edgar Lee. "Johnny Appleseed." In *Toward the Gulf*. New York: The Macmillan Co., 1918. See pages 42–45.

Sandburg, Carl. "Johnny Appleseed." *Chicago Daily News*, Oct. 20, 1926. Also published in *The People, Yes*. New York: Harcourt, Brace & World, 1936. See page 231.

Turner, Nancy Byrd. "Rhyme of Johnny Appleseed." *Child Life*, Aug. 28, 1937.

Music

Disney, Walt. *Melody Time*. Music and lyrics by Walter Kent and Kim Gannon, 1948.

Gaul, Harvey B. *Old Johnny Appleseed*. Cantata for treble voices. Boston: C. C. Birchard & Co., 1926.

Kettering, Eunice Lea. *In Praise of Johnny Appleseed*. Oratorio to poem by Vachel Lindsay, 1943.

Loomis, Harvey Worthington, and David Stevens. *Johnny Appleseed*. Operetta in one act for children. Cincinnati: Willis Music Co., 1925.

Siegmeister, Elie. "Johnny Appleseed." Lyric by Rosemary and Stephen Vincent Benét. In Olin Downes and Elie Siegmeister, eds. *Treasury of American Song*. New York: Howell, Soskin, & Co., 1940.

Wolfe, Jacques. "Johnny Appleseed." Lyric by Merrick F. McCarthy. For chorus of mixed voices, with baritone solo; also for high or low voice with piano accompaniment. New York: Carl Fischer, 1946.

Films and Audio/Visual Programs

Johnny Appleseed and the Frontier Within, 30 min., Swedenborg Foundation, 1989, VHS.

"Johnny Appleseed," from the Walt Disney Pictures *Melody Time*, 1948; VHS, 1998.

"Following the Footsteps of Johnny Appleseed," WVXU Radio, Cincinnati, Ohio, compact disc.

Commemorations

Commemorative Stamps

U. S. Postal Service commemorative postage stamp, first day covers issued at Leominster, Massachusetts, September 26, 1966.

Educational Programs and Organizations

Johnny Appleseed Heritage Center and Outdoor Historical Drama, Mansfield, Ohio

Johnny Appleseed's Outdoors, consortium of nonprofit Appleseed theme-related destinations, Mansfield, Ohio

Johnny Appleseed Society and Museum, Urbana University, Urbana, Ohio

Johnny Appleseed Workshop, sponsored by Johnny Appleseed Heritage Center, Inc., Mohican Outdoor School and Ashland University, Butler, Ohio

Johnny Appleseed Workshop, sponsored by Johnny Appleseed Society and Urbana University, Urbana, Ohio

Monuments, Markers, and Statues

Indiana

Fort Wayne

(1) Granite boulder in Swinney Park, gift of Hon. Stephen B. Fleming, erected by the Indiana Horticultural Society, 1916.

(2) Johnny Appleseed Memorial Park, including the Archer Burying Ground with the traditional site of John Chapman's grave. The site is marked by an iron fence, the gift of Hon. Stephen B. Fleming, 1916, and by a granite stone dedicated by the Optimist Club, May 26, 1935.

119

(3) Johnny Appleseed Memorial Bridge over St. Joseph River, dedicated May 21, 1949.

(4) Statue in Allen County Public Library, dedicated February 17, 1978.

(5) Johnny Appleseed Statue, Glen Brook Square Commons.

Massachusetts

Lancaster. Sculpture at Johnny Appleseed Visitor Center, dedicated September 7, 1998.

Leominster

(1) Granite marker at traditional site of John Chapman's birthplace, dedicated June 4, 1940.

(2) Sculpted head in Leominster Public Library, dedicated September 26, 1997.

(3) Sculpture in Johnny Appleseed School, dedicated September 26, 1997.

Springfield. Monument in Stebbins Park, erected by Springfield Garden Club, 1936.

Ohio

Allen County

(1) Allen County historic marker near Harter/Chapman lease, erected by the Allen County Historical Society, 1953.

(2) Allen County historic marker near an apple tree believed to be offspring of one planted by John Chapman, erected by the Allen County Historical Society, 1953.

Ashland

(1) Copus Massacre monument, Mifflin Township, Ashland County, dedicated by friends September 15, 1882.

(2) Monument erected by school children of Ashland County, dedicated July 28, 1915.

(3) Ohio Historic Marker below Charles Mill Dam, dedicated by Johnny Appleseed Heritage Center, Inc., September 15, 2000.

Athens. Stone and tablet dedicated by the Ohio Association of Garden Clubs; 1951.

Cincinnati. Statue in Spring Grove Cemetery, 1965.

Dexter City. Monument erected by the Johnny Appleseed Memorial Commission and the Washington County Pioneer Association, dedicated September 27, 1942.

Defiance. Stone marker near early nursery, dedicated by Defiance City Park Commission, 1941.

Mansfield

(1) Monument in Sherman-Heineman Middle Park, gift of Hon. M. B. Bushnell and dedicated by Richland Historical Society, Nov. 8, 1900. Rededicated with replacement monument and historic markers in South Park, Sept. 26, 1953.

(2) Ohio Historic Marker in Central Park, dedicated September 26, 1999, by Johnny Appleseed Heritage Center, Inc.; The Longaberger Co.; and the Ohio Bicentennial Commission.

Mount Blanchard. Stone marker at town lots, dedicated by Mount Blankhard Garden Club and Men's Garden Club of Findlay, 1966.

Mount Vernon

(1) Ohio Historic Marker near early nursery, dedicated by Knox County Historical Society, 1993.

(2) Ohio Historic Marker at town lots, dedicated September 26, 1999, by Johnny Appleseed Heritage Center, Inc.; The Longaberger Co.; and the Ohio Bicentennial Commission.

New Castle. Stone marker near early nursery, dedicated by New Castle Sesquicentennial and New Castle Township Trustees, 1961.

Pomeroy to Toledo. Johnny Appleseed Memorial Highway, State Routes 33, 31, and 25. Dedicated Sept. 28, 1950.

Pennsylvania

Franklin. Historic marker dedicated by the Pennsylvania Historical and Museum Commission, 1982.

Namesakes

J. Appleseed Press, San Francisco, California

Johnny Appleseed Chariot and Mural, Carousel, Mansfield, Ohio

Johnny Appleseed District, Heart of Ohio Boy Scouts of America, Mansfield, Ohio

Johnny Appleseed Junior High School, Mansfield, Ohio

Johnny Appleseed Mural, FirstMerit Bank, Mansfield, Ohio

Johnny Appleseed Orchard, Ashland, Ohio

Johnny Appleseed Park, Athens, Ohio

Johnny Appleseed Park District, Lima, Ohio

Johnny Appleseed Trail, Johnny Appleseed Boy Scouts District, Mansfield, Ohio

Johnny Appleseed Trail of North Central Massachusetts

Johnny Appleseed named Tree Planter of the Millennium, by Famous and Historic Trees, Jacksonville, Florida

William Ellery Jones is a scholar and lecturer who has spent decades researching the life and legend of John "Appleseed" Chapman. He is the founder and president of the Johnny Appleseed Heritage Center, Inc., and Johnny Appleseed Music, and executive producer of the Johnny Appleseed Outdoor Historical Drama, all in Mansfield, Ohio. He has lectured on the topic at universities, organizations, and churches.

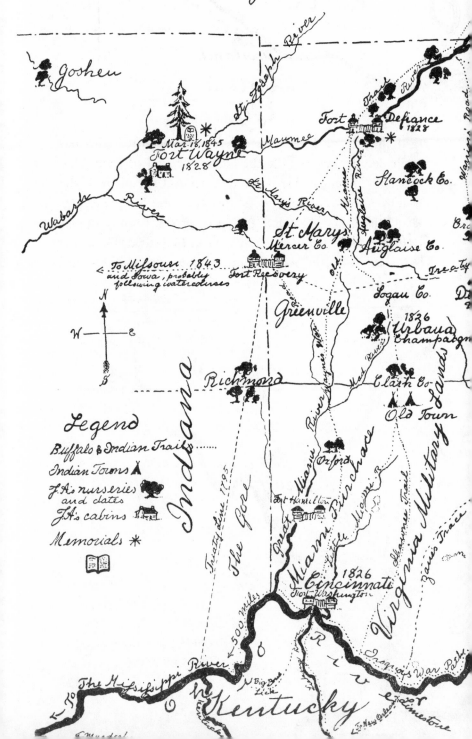

Michigan.

Goshen

Mar 18,1845
Fort Wayne
1828

St. Joseph River

Fort
Defiance
1828

Maumee

Hancock Co.

Wabash River

St. Mary's River

St. Marys
Mercer Co.

Auglaize Co.

Auglaize River

Maumee

Old

←To Missouri 1843
and Iowa, probably
following watercourses

Fort Recovery

Logan Co.

Treaty

Di

N

W   E

S

Greenville

River Wayne Trace

Urbana
Champaign

1826

Richmond

Mad River

Clark Co.

Old Town

Legend

Buffalo & Indian Trail ......

Indian Towns ▲

J. A.'s nurseries
and dates

J. A.'s cabins

Memorials ✳

Indiana

Treaty Line 1795

The Gore

Oxford

Great Miami River

Fort Hamilton

Little Miami R.

Miami Purchase

Shawnee Trail

Virginia Military Lands

Sans Trace

←500 miles

1826
Cincinnati
Fort Washington

←To The Mississippi River

Big Bone
Lick

Kentucky

Iroquois War Path

To New Orleans Limestone

Lake Erie

great Iroquois Trail

Cleveland

Western Reserve
(to Connecticut)

Sandusky

FIRE LANDS
Huron Co.
1811

*Ashland
Ashland Co

Fort Laurens

*Mansfield
Richland Co
1814

Mt Vernon
Knox Co.

Cos-hoc-ton

Newark

Licking
Road

Zanesville

Zane's Trace
old buffalo trail
Dexter City

Tuscarawas River

Seven Ranges

1806
Steubenville
Jefferson Co

Wheeling

To Potomac R.

Fort Duquesne Pittsburgh

Pennsylvania

Walhonding River

Muskingum River

Ohio Company

Chapman home 1805
Marietta

Blennerhasset Island

Ohio River

Virginia

Chillicothe

Chillicothe

Scioto River

O-Shingo Trail

La Salle

Kanawha River
670

"Johnny Appleseed"
his Map
of the Ohio Country
Compiled & sketched
by friends
1945